#CookFor SYRIA

RECIPE BOOK

CONTENTS

INTRODUCTION

#CookForSyria started off as an idea between two friends with a mutual love of food and a desire to help those in need.

Little did they know that a simple hashtag and a series of locally held events in London would lead to the beginnings of a global movement.

The campaign aims to increase awareness of the largest humanitarian crisis of our time, as well as raise the funds needed to aid children in Syria and the surrounding countries who have been displaced by war.

Since its inception, hundreds of people from different backgrounds and nationalities have shown their solidarity by joining this initiative – including top chefs, award-winning food writers and home cooks – cooking, baking and sharing Syrian-inspired dishes at their restaurants with their guests, at home with their friends and across social media with their fans and followers.

#CookForSyria has also provided a platform for Syrian families and those with a love of Middle Eastern cuisine to share recipes with each other, along with the stories behind those dishes.

This not-for-profit book is a collection of 100 recipes and photographs lovingly donated by those who have come together for a common cause.

It includes:

- Traditional dishes, donated by Syrian families who have handed them down between generations.

- Modern recipes with a Syrian-inspired twist, donated by top chefs, celebrated restaurants and award-winning cookbook authors.

- Tips on how to host your own charity event (including a supper club or a bake sale).

From za'atar flatbreads served with a Muhammara dip subtly spiced with aleppo pepper to a fragrant orange blossom and milk pudding, these dishes are designed for sharing with loved ones and new friends.

The recipes included in this book are by no means a definitive guide to Syrian cuisine, but they aim to shine a spotlight on some of the incredible dishes from this once peaceful and beautiful country.

"We've been overwhelmed by the support and kindness of everyone involved in this initiative. Food has the power to bring people together. Our hope is that these recipes will be passed on to others and will inspire as many people as possible to #CookForSyria."

Clerkenwell Boy & Serena Guen

A MESSAGE FROM SYRIA

Thank you for your generous contribution to the children of Syria. By purchasing this #CookForSyria recipe book, you are helping these children to overcome their suffering and realise their dreams.

Since the onset of the crisis in Syria in 2011, violence throughout the country has continued, violating the most basic principles of international humanitarian, human and child rights laws, affecting the lives of millions of children and their families.

Indiscriminate attacks on schools and hospitals, using water as a weapon of war, child recruitment and access restrictions on delivering humanitarian assistance to those in need are among the many violations being practiced against children and their families. Unicef has been at the forefront in protecting and advancing the rights of every boy and girl in Syria since the outset of the crisis. To help these children and their families better cope with their dire situation, and to further enhance their resilience, Unicef provides access to safe water; healthcare and nutrition services; an education and protection from violence, exploitation and abuse.

In Syria, as children face a world that endlessly challenges their aspirations, they continue to demonstrate determination, resilience and hope. I have witnessed this in the dreams of every girl or boy I have met. All children have one wish in common – to continue their education and become the future teachers, architects and physicians who will rebuild a better Syria.

A global commitment to protecting these children's rights can pull their lives back from the brink, and unleash their full potential. By buying this #CookForSyria recipe book, you will help children who are at greatest need for your support, for which we are deeply grateful. Your generous and valuable support will help us to not leave even one child behind.

Fran Equiza
Unicef Syria Representative

WHY SYRIA?

Syria is one of the most dangerous place to be a child. After six years of war, 6 million children inside Syria are in urgent need of humanitarian assistance – 12 times more than in 2012. 2.5 million children are now living as refugees in neighbouring Turkey, Lebanon, Jordan, Egypt and Iraq.

One in three Syrian children have grown up knowing only crisis. Their young lives have been shaped by danger, fear and insecurity – and with the crisis showing no signs of stopping, the number is only going to get higher.

Violence is everywhere, ripping apart places that children thought were safe – places that should be safe: schools, hospitals, playgrounds, public parks and family homes.

Unicef, the world's leading children's organisation, is working tirelessly to protect Syrian children and give them hope for a happy future. They are inside Syria and in the refugee camps, ensuring children have access to life-saving food, water and medical care. But they are also providing longer term support to help children, young people and families rebuild their lives. They're providing education, psychosocial support and safe spaces for them to play and have some much-needed fun.

In 2016, Unicef helped to provide almost 15 million Syrians with access to safe drinking water. Their psychosocial support programmes helped more than 500,000 Syrian children cope with the horrors they have experienced. Inside Syria itself, they provided more than 3 million children with essential learning supplies and helped to reach more than 850,000 children with polio vaccinations. Unicef will do whatever it takes until every child is safe.

A child is a child, no matter what. All children need a safe home and hope for a happy future. By supporting #CookForSyria, you're helping Unicef be there for the children of Syria.

HOW TO GET INVOLVED

MAKING A DIFFERENCE HAS NEVER TASTED SO GOOD, AND IT'S SO EASY TO TAKE PART

HOST
Anyone can host their own #CookForSyria supper club to fundraise for Unicef's Syria Appeal. You could have a #CookForSyria breakfast, lunch or dinner. Ask your guests to donate at the door or set up your own JustGiving page for those who want to donate later (no cash required!). You could also organise a #BakeForSyria charity cake sale at your office, university or school.

ATTEND
Restaurants are participating and events are popping up all over the world. Check out our website to see the latest in your area.

START #COOKFORSYRIA IN YOUR CITY
If #CookForSyria isn't happening in your hometown and you want to do something about it, then let us know by emailing hello@coofkorsyria.com and we'll see what we can do.

More information visit CookForSyria.com

SHARE
The Syrian cooking tradition is one of the oldest in the world and reflects the country's rich cultural heritage, with influences from across the Middle East and beyond. Whether you've cooked for Syria, eaten at one of our partner restaurants or just want to repost beautiful images of Syrian-inspired dishes, we are asking you all to spread the word.

Share the love
@CookForSyria
#CookForSyria
@NextGenLondon
@UNICEF_UK

HOW TO HOST A #COOKFORSYRIA CHARITY BREAKFAST, BRUNCH, LUNCH OR DINNER

Donated by Jackson&Levine
@IAmLauraJackson @ThisIsAliceLevine
@JacksonAndLevine

From intimate dinners in their East London home to whimsical evenings held in a hidden tile factory on Regent's Canal, Alice Levine and Laura Jackson, aka Jackson&Levine, have thrown their fair share of supper clubs. Laura even hosted our #CookForSyria launch dinner in London with Rosie Birkett (see the salads and vegetables chapter for Rosie's mujadara recipe). Here, the experts give their tips on hosting your own #CookForSyria charity breakfast, brunch, lunch or dinner.

Family style

Syrian food is all about sharing with others. Serving dishes "family style" on large platters will create a great atmosphere, particularly between people who don't know each other.

Set the scene

When it comes to table design, expensive is not always best. For our recent supper club, we made our own serving boards from recycled wood. We tend to spend nearly as much time transforming the space as we do on the food – you want guests to have a memorable experience as well as a great meal. Handwritten menus and invitations with information about the charity you are supporting will also add a personal touch.

Discover local finds

Always keep your eyes peeled, wherever you are! We have found some great pieces including serving platters and glassware in charity shops, and love a holiday market for interesting tableware. For our last supper club, we went foraging on Hackney Marshes and discovered some beautiful pink sweet pea flowers (we do, however, advise you to follow foraging guidelines).

Music

Spend some time on the playlist. Something that suits the feel and style of the event. What's on the record player will set the mood.

Keep it simple

Have at least one cold course. This can be a starter (such as some of the dips and flatbreads from the mezze chapter of this recipe book), a beautiful salad to share or a stunning dessert made in advance. This will give you more time to relax and speak with guests, and can be a lifesaver for those with a small oven and kitchen.

Slow cooking

Preparing dishes a few hours in advance can help you feel more organised and add a greater depth of flavour. An inexpensive cut of meat can be delicious, especially when slow cooked (see the soups and stews chapter for ideas). Your butcher can advise where to get bang for your buck.

The little things

Be generous with your leftovers. If you have lots of lovely flatbread left, wrap it up in greaseproof paper with a bow and give it to guests for breakfast the next day. You could even put some of the amazing Syrian spices into pouches with recipe cards for your guests to use at their own Syrian supper clubs. It's the little touches that people remember.

Get social

And, of course, share your experience and encourage others to #CookForSyria.

Photography by @KatieWilsonFoto
Portrait by @JamesAGrant
Styling by @KloellaDeville

STORE CUPBOARD ESSENTIALS

ALEPPO CHILLI

Hailing from the Silk Road spice route, these rich red peppers are both gentle and fragrant. They are dried, deseeded and ground into coarse flakes that add a mild heat to any dish.

BAHARAT

Baharat is a popular, all-purpose spice used across the Middle East. If you can't buy it, then it's quite easy to make your own to taste using allspice, black peppercorns, cinnamon, coriander seeds, cloves, nutmeg and paprika. A little goes a long way.

BULGUR WHEAT

This comes in several varieties and tends to be utilised in soups and salads, as well as for kibbeh dishes.

CHICKPEAS

A versatile ingredient that can be used in dips (such as hummus), snacks (such as falafel) and larger dishes (such as fatteh).

DATES

Perfect in both sweet and savoury dishes, we especially love medjool dates (often described as "the king of dates"). They are large and soft in texture, with a beautiful caramel and honey flavour profile. Date syrup is often used in dishes to add a layer of sweetness.

FLATBREAD

Flatbreads are an essential part of any Syrian meal and are great for dipping into hummus, soups and stews, or when used in fattoush (bread salad). Many of the #CookForSyria recipe book contributors have provided recipes for their favourite flatbread.

GARLIC

Widely used in various dips and marinades, we especially love the combination of garlic, lemon and broad beans in Dalia Dogmoch Soubra's foul Moukala recipe.

HALLOUMI

Popular all across the Middle East and Mediterranean, halloumi is a semi-hard cheese and tastes best when grilled or fried. Try serving with a drizzle of honey and poached figs.

KEBAB SKEWERS

Essential for cooking dishes from the Middle East, it's worth investing in some good-quality reusable metal skewers whether you plan to grill your kebabs outside on the barbecue or in the kitchen (but be careful not to burn your fingers).

LABNEH

A fresh cheese made from yoghurt that has been strained to remove its whey, resulting in a thicker consistency. Perfect for spreading on flatbread, or rolled into a ball and dipped in various herbs and spices.

MINT

Dried mint is used in many recipes and marinades – it also makes the perfect coating for our easy-to-make labneh balls.

NUTS

Syrian families love serving toasted pine nuts with fragrant rice, mixing pistachios with salads and cakes or blending together walnuts for the most delicious muhammara pepper dip.

ORANGE BLOSSOM WATER

Made from the distilled blossoms of orange trees, this intense and fragrant liquid can be used in syrups, cakes, rice puddings and baklavas.

POMEGRANATE

The jewel-like, ruby-coloured flesh of pomegranates can transform everyday dishes into something special.

ROSEWATER

One of the most famous flowers in the world, the Damask rose has been used for centuries in the Middle East and beyond to flavour desserts and sweet treats.

SUMAC

Sumac is a rich, burgundy-coloured spice with a distinctive lemony flavour. It tastes great with salads and grilled meats, and is also delicious sprinkled over hummus.

TAHINI

Tahini is a paste made from ground sesame seeds. It has a distinctive taste and is used in dips, sauces and to complement savoury dishes – but also works well with cakes and desserts.

YOGHURT

An essential and versatile ingredient used for mezze, salads, main courses and desserts.

ZA'ATAR

Za'atar is an intensely aromatic spice blend traditionally made with dried herbs such as marjoram or thyme (the Arabic word za'atar also means thyme). It is commonly used on flatbreads or to flavour meat and vegetable dishes.

Pancakes

Eggs

To share

I. BREAKFAST & BRUNCH

"A simple bowl at sunrise with just a handful of basic ingredients can be comforting and delicious."

Symmetry Breakfast

ATAYEF (PANCAKES) WITH RICOTTA, DATES & CARDAMOM HONEY V

Donated by John Whaite
@JohnWhaiteBakes

"This dish was inspired by the communality of food. Pancakes, for example, cross borders and religions – from Easter to Eid."

Serves 8-10

For the batter
55g plain flour
a pinch of salt
2 large eggs
115ml whole milk
sunflower oil, for frying

For the filling
175g stoned dates
175g ricotta
zest of 1 small orange

For the frying and honey
750ml sunflower oil
200g runny honey
3 cardamom pods, bruised
50g pistachio nuts, roughly crushed

This whole campaign is about recognising and embracing humanity, as well as the need for us all to protect that beautiful thing that we take for granted: life. And food is the ultimate giver of life.

To make the batter, mix together the flour and salt in a small bowl. Make a well in the centre, crack in the eggs and add a good splash of the milk. Whisk the ingredients together to form a smooth, thick batter, then slowly add the rest of the milk, whisking.

Before you cook the pancakes, dampen a clean tea towel to cover the pancakes – it's important that they don't dry out.

In a good non-stick frying pan, heat a small amount of oil over a high heat. Once the pan starts to haze, reduce the heat to medium/low. Add a tablespoon of batter, spread to a disk of about four inches in diameter, and allow to cook just until the upper surface becomes dull and satiny, and pinprick bubbles appear – about 30 seconds. Using a pallete knife or fish slice, lift the pancake on to a large plate – cooked side down – and cover with the tea towel. Repeat until you have used all the batter – you may need to add a little more oil to the pan every five or six pancakes.

To make the filling, chop the dates, as finely as is humanly possible – though I prefer the mechanical help of a food processor. Beat together with the ricotta and zest to form a thick paste.

Take a pancake in your hand, cooked side down in the palm, and place a heaped teaspoon of the filling onto the centre. Fold the pancake in half, encasing the filling, and pinch the meeting edges together firmly – rather like a pixie-sized pasty.

To fry, heat the oil in a heavy-based saucepan or wok, until it reaches 180C/355F, or until a cube of bread sizzles frantically when dropped in. Add the atayefs, four at a time, and fry until a medium/dark golden brown. Remove from the oil and drain on a piece of kitchen towel.

For the honey drizzle, heat the honey and cardamom in a small saucepan until very runny.

To serve, dip or drench the atayef in the honey, then top with pistachio pieces.

Photography by @JohnWhaiteBakes

DAMASCENE PANCAKES, TOPPED WITH GRAPE MOLASSES & TAHINI V

Donated by Itab Azzam and Dina Mousawi of Syria Recipes From Home
@ItabAzzam @DMousawi @Syria_RecipesFromHome

"We learned to make this dish with Syrian women that we met for our book Syria: Recipes from Home." - Dina and Itab.

Makes approximately 14 pancakes

For the pancakes
200g plain flour
300ml warm milk
a pinch of yeast
a pinch of baking powder
a pinch of sugar
vegetable oil, for frying

For the topping
2 bananas, sliced
grape molasses
tahini
sesame seeds, toasted

These are a speciality of Damascus, traditionally sold by a man on a bicycle, who would cycle around neighbourhoods with a glass box attached to the back of his bike. The box is filled with these treats that people would devour on the spot. Grapes are grown all over Syria and you could say grape molasses is the Maple Syrup of our country.

In a blender combine all the pancake ingredients and blend until you have a smooth texture with bubbles.

Leave to rest for 10 minutes, then blend again.

Pour a ladle of the mixture into a hot frying pan and cook for a couple of minutes before flipping it and cooking the other side.

Top with sliced bananas and then generously drizzle with grape molasses, tahini and a sprinkle of toasted sesame seeds. Eat immediately.

Photography by @KatieWilsonFoto
Styling by @KloellaDeville
With thanks to Backgrounds Prop Hire

HERBY PANCAKES WITH BAHARAT-SPICED ROASTED VEGETABLES, LABNEH, ALEPPO PEPPER OIL & PISTACHIO & PINK PEPPERCORN DUKKAH V

Donated by Lyndell Sabine and Scarlett Dixon of Crumble.
@CrumbleFood

Serves 4

For the labneh
150g thick greek yoghurt
5g salt

For the roasted vegetables
1 butternut squash, peeled, deseeded and chopped
1 courgette, chopped
1 aubergine, chopped
1 cauliflower, chopped
30-45g baharat spice blend
75ml olive oil
5g turmeric
1 tsp salt

For the herby pancakes (soccas)
1 bunch parsley
1 bunch coriander
1 bunch dill
1 bunch chives
75ml olive oil
1 tsp turmeric
240g chickpea flour
470ml water
1 tsp baking powder
2 tsp salt

For the dukkah
70g unsalted pistachios, shelled
1 tsp fennel seeds
1 tbsp cumin seeds
1 tbsp pink peppercorns, dried
3 tbsp coriander seeds
½ tsp nigella seeds
½ tsp maldon sea salt
1 tsp paprika

For the aleppo pepper oil
10g aleppo pepper
60ml olive oil

This recipe was inspired by our friend who produced the documentary about the White Helmets [the Syrian Civil Defence] for Netflix. The number of steps looks long, but they are simple steps so you'll whizz through. The recipe will give you leftover herb oil, aleppo pepper oil, roasted vegetables and dukkah – but they are all useful things to have lying around.

To make the labneh, combine the greek yoghurt and salt and spoon the mix into a cloth placed in a sieve over a bowl. Leave it in the fridge overnight. If you don't have time, then just use thick greek yoghurt.

Heat the oven to 200C/400F/gas 6. Arrange the butternut squash, courgette and aubergine in a roasting dish in a single layer with 45ml of olive oil, the baharat mix and half a teaspoon of salt and roast for 15-20 minutes. Remove from the oven, then turn up to 240C/475F/gas 9.

Mix the cauliflower with the turmeric, the remaining oil and salt. Roast for 5 minutes.

Next, you need to make the herb oil. Blend the herbs, olive oil and 1 teaspoon of salt until you have a smooth, thick paste.

For the socca batter, whisk the chickpea flour with the water, baking powder and the other teaspoon of salt until it is the consistency of pancake mixture. Leave it to rest.

For the dukkah, dry-toast the pistachios for 3-5 minutes in a pan on a medium heat. Add the fennel, cumin, pink peppercorns and coriander to the pan and toast for another minute or two. Crush in a pestle and mortar. Add the nigella, paprika and salt and stir. Store in an airtight jar.

Next, for the aleppo pepper oil, mix the oil and the pepper and store in an airtight jar.

To make the soccas, heat a tablespoon of olive oil in a small, non-stick frying pan on a medium heat. Stir through 2-3 tbsp of the herb oil into the batter until it is a uniform green colour.

Ladle some batter into the hot frying pan so that it comes about ¾cm up the side. When bubbles appear, flip it until it is nicely coloured on both sides. Repeat until you have 4 pancakes.

To serve, place some vegetables on top of the pancake, followed by a dollop of labneh. Drizzle some aleppo pepper oil, sprinkle on a good amount of the dukkah and then dot a little of the remaining herb oil on the plate.

Photography by @KatieWilsonFoto
Styling by @KloellaDeville

ÇILBIR (POACHED EGGS, CHILLI BUTTER & YOGHURT) V

Donated by Hus Vedat at Yosma
@HusVedat @Yosma_London

Serves 1

2 burford brown eggs
a splash of wine vinegar
2 leeks
1 tsp parsley oil
salt
pepper
2 tbsp strained yoghurt
garlic, finely crushed
10ml ginger, juiced
75-100g butter
aleppo pepper

There are records of çılbır being eaten by Ottoman sultans as far back as the 15th century. It is now common to serve the dish topped with melted butter infused with aleppo pepper. Here's my take.

Crack the eggs on to a plate with a little wine vinegar. Gently drop into 90C/195F water, swirling every so often. Take out once cooked to your preference.

Cook the leeks directly on hot coals until blackened. Peel off the first layer, chop, then season with salt and pepper and parsley oil.

Add the garlic and ginger juice to the yoghurt and mix.

For the chilli butter, put some butter in a pan and melt but do not brown. Add a generous amount of aleppo pepper. Remove from the heat and stir until the pepper has infused the butter. Pass through a sieve.

Assemble the dish.

Photography by @CharlotteHuCo

OJJI WITH YOGHURT & MINT DIP V

Donated by Shirin Kouros and Yasmine Larizadeh
at The Good Life Eatery
@GoodLifeEatery

"The most interesting part of our research into Syrian cuisine was seeing the various influences and notes of Persian flavours, our heritage, here at The Good Life Eatery."

Makes 15 small ojji

300g courgettes, grated
75g spring onions, finely chopped
300g self-raising flour (or 300g plain flour and 1 tbsp baking soda)
6 medium eggs
40g parsley, roughly chopped
40g coriander, roughly chopped
3 cloves garlic, crushed
2 tsp red chilli flakes
2 tsp salt
vegetable or sunflower oil, for frying

For the yoghurt and mint dip

250g thick yoghurt or labneh
1 tbsp mint, dried
2-3 pinches of salt, to taste

To serve

10 spring onion garnishes
flatbread

Having a Middle Eastern background, we have grown up with many various nationalities from the region. I had a Syrian friend in high school and I always remember eating something her mother would make us when we would go to her home to study after school. After ringing her, she reminded me that the delicious morsels of warmth were called Ojji. She said it was very traditional, and something she grew up eating regularly at home. I spent some time researching this dish which I had never tried to make, and found almost nothing online about it ... rather curious. After asking around, I managed to get my hands on a recipe. Hope you like our twist. We have added coriander, red chilli flakes and some spring onion inside of the pancake to freshen up the flavours.

Wash and towel-dry the courgettes, spring onions, parsley and coriander to remove any grit or dirt.

In a large metal bowl, grate the courgette using a coarse grater.

In the same bowl, combine all the ingredients except for the flour and mix well with a fork. Add the flour by generously sprinkling it over the mixture, stirring in slowly to ensure that there are no flour lumps. The mix should be quite thick.

Heat a large frying pan with 2-3 tablespoons of oil on a medium heat. Using a large spoon or a ladle, dollop the mixture into the pan to form small fritters. Fry on one side until golden and then flip over on to the other side and cook until golden. Continue the process until you have made all the pancakes. The ojji can be eaten warm or at room temperature.

To make the dip, combine the yoghurt with the mint and the salt in a small bowl.

Serve the ojji with the yoghurt dip, the spring onion garnishes and flatbread.

Photography by @tilfrances

SUMAC-CURED PRAWN OMELETTE WITH ALEPPO CHILLI SAMBAL

Donated by Anna Hansen at The Modern Pantry
@TheModernPantry

"It is hard not to be aware of the suffering happening in Syria on a day-to-day to basis, but what I find most inspiring, apart from the wealth of interesting spices and herbs, is that the focus of the cuisine is sharing. Food is a way of bringing people together."

Serves 4

For the sumac-cured prawns

18 prawns, peeled, split lengthways and de-veined
1 lemongrass stalk, bashed gently with a rolling pin, or other suitable implement, and chopped into 4 pieces
30g ginger, peeled and sliced
3 kaffir lime leaves, shredded
1 tsp aleppo chilli flakes, dried
1 tbsp soy sauce
1 tbsp fish sauce (nam pla)
2 tsp sumac
100g white sugar
15g maldon sea salt

For the aleppo chilli sambal

2.5 litres of rapeseed oil, for frying
250g onions, sliced
250g ripe cherry tomatoes, quartered, with the seeds removed
80g tender confit garlic
80g fresh ginger, cut into fine strips
25g dried shrimps, ground finely in a spice grinder
1 tsp chipotle chilli flakes
½ tsp aleppo chilli flakes
1 tsp sweet smoked paprika
100g tamarind paste
30g pomegranate molasses
40ml fish sauce

For the omelettes

12 eggs
3 tsp smoked chilli sambal
butter, for frying
1 bunch spring onions, sliced
1 green chilli, sliced into super-fine rounds
1 bunch coriander

This is a classic from our menu, in fact it's one of our most popular dishes, and it works really well with a hint of heat, so I was inspired to adapt this element for the campaign. The idea was to create awareness and conversation, so I chose a dish that everyone already knows and loves to maximise that potential. It made perfect sense to give it a Syrian element by using aleppo chillies instead of standard red chillies. The flavour is richer and has more depth, in fact I think I will keep using the aleppo chilli. I have also used pomegranate molasses for acidity in the sambal and cured the prawns with a little sumac.

To cure the prawns, mix all the ingredients together well and leave to marinate for 24 hours, then rinse and pat dry. Store in an airtight container in the fridge until ready to serve. They should keep for 6 days.

For the sambal, heat the oil in a deep-fat fryer to 180C/355F, then deep-fry the onions and cherry tomatoes separately in small batches until they are a deep golden brown – almost burnt looking – draining them on paper towel and then tipping them into a large bowl as you go. Deep-fry the ginger and garlic, also in separate batches, until just golden brown.

In a small frying pan, fry the ground shrimps in a little of the leftover deep-frying oil until aromatic. Add to the bowl along with all the remaining ingredients and mix thoroughly.

Now blitz the mixture in batches in a food processor until almost smooth, emptying it out into another bowl as you go. Once you have done this, mix the processed sambal together thoroughly and allow to cool. Place in an airtight container and refrigerate until needed.

For each omelette, whisk two eggs together in a small bowl with ½ a teaspoon of sambal. The sambal provides the seasoning, so avoid the urge to add salt. Heat a knob of butter in an omelette pan over a moderate heat, and when it begins to sizzle, add 6 prawn halves.

Toss these in the pan until almost cooked, then pour in the eggs. Swirl the pan once or twice, then reduce the heat. Sprinkle over 3 green chilli rounds and a small handful of spring onions. When the eggs look almost cooked, use a flat heatproof rubber spatula to fold the omelette in half.

Slide on to a plate and keep somewhere warm while you repeat the process. To serve, garnish with coriander leaves and a spoonful of the sambal.

Photography by @PatriciaNiven

SLOW-COOKED SPICED LAMB SHOULDER WITH BUTTERMILK & CORIANDER

Donated by Ben Tish at Salt Yard Group
@Ben.Tish @SaltYardGroup

Serves 6-7

1 lamb shoulder (approximately 3 kg), bone in and fat side scored with a very sharp knife

50ml olive oil

3 tbsp paprika, smoked

4 tbsp coriander seeds, crushed

2 tbsp cumin, ground

8 garlic cloves, roughly chopped

50ml red wine vinegar

sea salt

black pepper

For the dressing

100ml buttermilk

20ml white wine vinegar

½ bunch fresh coriander, chopped

A favourite of mine, this style of spicing works harmoniously with lamb. Well they have been doing it for centuries. I do this in an oven and on a barbecue as well, both work incredibly well and both benefit from a good long marinade, preferably overnight.

Lay out a large double layer of foil and place the lamb on top. Pour over the oil and then rub in plenty of seasoning along with the paprika, cumin, garlic and coriander, then drizzle over the vinegar. Rub the meat all over and massage the spices into the flesh.

Wrap up the foil to completely cover the meat and place in the fridge for at least 5 hours, or overnight. Remove the lamb from the fridge and place on an oven tray.
Heat an oven to 180C/350F/gas 4. Place the lamb in the oven and cook for 2 hours with the foil on, then remove the foil, baste the meat with the juices and cook for a further hour to caramelise.

Check the meat, you should be able to easily pull the flesh away from the bone and cut it with a spoon. If it is still firm, turn the temperature down to 150C/300F/gas 2 and cook for a further 40 minutes. Remove from the oven and rest for 30 minutes before serving.

While it is resting, whisk together the buttermilk, vinegar and coriander and season to taste. Remove the bone from the shoulder and serve whole at the table for people to help themselves along with the dressing. Or pull apart the meat, season and serve on top of grilled flatbread.

Photography by @PatriciaNiven

LAHAM BAJINE SYRIAN PIZZA

Donated by James Elliot at Pizza Pilgrims
@PizzaPilgrims

"I found that the food is AMAZING in Syria! Beautifully spiced and bizarrely using a lot of the same ingredients as Italy."

Serves 4-5

For the dough
1kg high-gluten 00 flour
2g fresh baker's yeast
700ml cold water
30g table salt

For the topping
1 medium onion, diced
500g ground beef
70g tomato puree
mozzarella
basil
chicken stock
natural yoghurt
½ tsp cumin
½ tsp turmeric
1 tsp coriander
¼ tsp allspice
¼ tsp cinnamon
¼ tsp black pepper
salt, to taste
a good pinch of za'atar spice mix

The flatbreads from the Middle East are some of the best in the world and Syria actually has its own style of pizza called Laham Bajine. Our version is inspired by this, and also a little by manoushe breads from Lebanon. The only changes we've made are using our Neapolitan pizza dough and adding mozzarella. The za'atar spice mix is very common in Syrian cuisine.

To make the dough, tip the flour on to your work surface and make a well in the centre. Dissolve your yeast in the water and pour into the middle of the well a little at a time, while using your hands to bring the walls of the flour in so that the water begins to thicken.

Once you've reached the consistency of custard, add the salt and bring in the rest of the flour until it comes together as a dough. Knead for 10-15 minutes until firm. Cover and leave to rest for 10 minutes before kneading again quickly for 10 seconds. (This helps to develop the flavour and the gluten.)

Divide the dough into 200g balls and leave to rest overnight, or for at least 8 hours (24 hours is optimal, 48 hours is the maximum) in a sealed container or a deep baking dish sprinkled with flour and covered in clingfilm. Remember to leave space for each of your dough balls because, as the gluten relaxes, they will spread out to take up twice the diameter that they do initially.

For the topping, brown off the beef mince in a heavy-bottomed pan in a tablespoon of olive oil. Add the onion and continue to fry off for 5-10 minutes until the onions have softened. Add all the spices and cook through for 2-3 minutes.

Stir in the tomato puree and pour over the chicken stock. Simmer on a low heat for 45-60 minutes with the lid on until the meat has softened and the sauce has reduced. (You may have to add water from time to time to stop it from drying out.) Turn off the heat and leave to cool.

Spread a good spoonful of the mixture on to your pizza base and top with mozzarella and basil. Bake in the hottest oven you can find, or use our frying pan technique on our website.

Finish with natural yoghurt and a good pinch of the za'atar spice mix.

Photography by @Joe_Woodhouse

LAMB & POMEGRANATE FLATBREADS

Donated by Sophie Michell
@SophieMichell

"These dishes were inspired by my time living in Beirut, back when Syria was absolutely seen as a safe haven as the political situation in Lebanon worsened. I love the flavours from this part of the world, I find the food in Syria is so beautiful and romantic."

Makes 8 topped flatbreads

For the bread

400g strong bread flour, plus extra for dusting

1 medium free-range egg, beaten

250g yoghurt

3 tbsp olive oil, plus extra for oiling

sea salt

For the lamb topping

1 tbsp olive oil

1 onion, finely chopped

2 garlic cloves, finely chopped

400g minced lamb

½ tsp cinnamon, ground

a pinch of cumin, ground

a pinch of coriander, ground

1 tbsp tomato puree

1 tbsp pomegranate molasses, plus extra to drizzle (optional)

To serve

3 tbsp pine nuts

a small handful of chopped mint

100g pomegranate seeds

These are served as a breakfast on the go or as a snack all over the Middle East, especially in Syria and its neighbour Lebanon. For a vegetarian and quicker version, omit the lamb mix and spread the rolled-out discs with za'atar and olive oil, then bake. Za'atar is an aromatic spice mix that is used a lot. Everyone has their own version, but generally it is a combination of sumac, thyme and toasted sesame seeds.

For the flatbreads, mix the flour, egg, yoghurt and olive oil together in a medium bowl. Season with salt and knead to form a smooth dough. Cover and chill in the fridge until needed.

For the lamb topping, heat the oil in a large saucepan over a medium heat, add the onion, garlic and lamb and stir until well combined. Cook for 10 minutes, stirring occasionally, until the ingredients start to turn golden and come together.

Add the spices, cook for a few more minutes, then add the tomato puree and season with salt and pepper. Stir in the pomegranate molasses, then remove the pan from the heat.

Preheat the oven to 180C/350F/gas 4.

Take the flatbread dough from the fridge and turn it out on to a lightly floured surface. Roll the dough into a ball, then divide it into 8 pieces (for medium-sized flatbreads) or 24 pieces (for bite-sized flatbreads).

Roll each piece into a circle, flatten it with the heel of your hand and then roll into a thin disc with a rolling pin. Place the discs on to baking trays and spread some of the lamb mixture over the top, then bake for 15 minutes until crisp and golden.

Remove from the oven and serve topped with the pine nuts, mint and pomegranate seeds. Drizzle the lamb flatbreads with the extra pomegranate molasses.

Photography by @PatriciaNiven

ZA'ATAR FLATBREADS WITH HONEY-POACHED FIGS & GRILLED HALLOUMI V

Donated by Sophie Michell
@SophieMichell

"It is heartbreaking to see how Syria is being torn apart. The refugees that we see on the news can seem so distant to us, when in fact they are normal people trying to make their lives work – just like you or I."

Makes 8 flatbreads

For the bread

400g strong bread flour, plus extra for dusting

1 medium free-range egg, beaten

250g yoghurt

3 tbsp olive oil, plus extra for mixing with the za'atar topping

sea salt

150g za'atar

For the poached figs

8 medium deep-purple figs, trimmed

150g honey

150ml water

a splash of orange-blossom water (optional)

8 thick slices of halloumi or akkawi cheese

This dish conjures up Levantine memories for me – the smells, the feel and the vibe. That part of the world will always be engraved in my mind after living there, and I do miss the heady energy and magic. Make this as part of a large mezze or a breakfast. It's very moreish and very lovely. The Syrian aspects of this dish are all very classic, however, when I am in the Middle East I use akkawi cheese, which is very similar to halloumi and an absolute fave out there.

For the flatbreads, mix the flour, egg, yoghurt and olive oil together in a medium bowl. Season with salt and knead to form a smooth dough. Cover and chill in the fridge until needed.

While the dough is resting, poach the figs. Bring the water and honey up to a rolling boil in a small saucepan, then add the the figs and simmer for 5 minutes until tender. Take out the figs and pop on to a plate, then place the liquid back on to the stove and reduce until syrupy. (Add a splash of orange-blossom water at this point if using.) When the liquid has a syrupy consistency, take off the heat and add the figs back in.

Preheat the oven to 180C/350F/gas 4.

Take the flatbread dough from the fridge and turn it out on to a lightly floured surface. Roll the dough into a ball, then divide into 8 pieces (for medium-sized flatbreads) or 24 pieces (for bite-sized flatbreads). Roll each piece into a circle, flatten it with the heel of your hand and then roll into a thin disc with a rolling pin. Mix 150g of za'atar with a good splash of olive oil and brush over the discs, sprinkling over some sea salt. Place the discs on to baking trays, and then bake for 15 minutes until crisp and golden.

While the flatbreads are cooking, heat a griddle pan or frying pan to a high temperature, rub the slices of cheese with oil and then griddle or fry the cheese for a few minutes on each side until golden on the outside and soft in the middle.

Then serve some slices of cheese, two figs and some flatbreads to each person, or put everything on a big platter in the middle of the table to share.

Photography by @PatriciaNiven

LAMB BURGER WITH BRAISED LAMB SHOULDER, FETA SAUCE, & ALEPPO PEPPER RELISH

Donated by Luke Findlay at Patty & Bun
@TheGravySocial @PattyAndBun

"Like in every Arabic culture, I discovered just how important food is for a sense of community in Syria. I like how everybody eats together and that women aren't segregated when it comes to eating like in a lot of other cultures."

Serves 6-8

For the lamb shoulder
1 boned-out lamb shoulder
2 spanish onions
12 garlic cloves
20g sweet paprika
10g cumin, ground
20g coriander, ground
30g sumac
180ml pomegranate molasses

For the chilli relish
10g aleppo chillies, dried
3 fresh aleppo chillies (pul biber)
40g pickled red onion
5g sumac
10g pomegranate molasses
¼ bunch flat-leaf parsley
3 tomatoes
5g kosher salt

For the feta and garlic sauce
180g feta
1 clove garlic
20g olive oil

6-8 burger buns
6-8 lamb patties, cooked to taste

I was inspired to make this dish by the Syrians' love for shawarma, which is on every street corner there, and is staple of life. The main elements I've used are the use of aleppo chillies and pomegranate molasses, which are everyday ingredients in Syria.

For the braised lamb shoulder, preheat the oven to 160C/325F/gas 3. Break the lamb shoulder down into 5 chunks and season with salt. In a large pan, sear the lamb on all sides until golden brown. Remove the lamb and set aside.

Finely dice the onions and add to the pan. Slowly sweat the onions, then finely slice the garlic and add to the pan. Once the onions and the garlic have softened, add the spices and cook out for 5 minutes.

Put the lamb back in the pan and add the pomegranate molasses. Cover with water. Put a lid on the pan and cook in the oven for about 4 hours, or until the meat is falling apart.

Remove the meat from the pan and flake. Reduce the sauce so that it coats the back of a spoon. Add the meat back to the sauce and check for seasoning.

For the relish, char the fresh chillies using a blowtorch or over the flame of a gas hob. Scrape out the seeds and finely dice. Then finely dice the tomatoes and the pickled onions and finely chop the parsley. Mix all the ingredients in a bowl and check for seasoning.

For the feta and garlic sauce, blitz the garlic and olive oil together in a food processor until the mix has emulsified. Break up the feta and add to the food processor. Then whip the sauce until it has a smooth, glossy texture. Cook the patties to taste and assemble your burgers with the shoulder, relish and sauce.

Photography by @MillyKR

FATTEH V

Donated by Michael Zee of Symmetry Breakfast
@SymmetryBreakfast

"Syrian cuisine is very family specific, comparing recipes from many sources reveals just how many twists and turns the same dish can make."

Serves 2

- 2 pitta breads
- 2 tbsp olive oil
- 4 tbsp light tahini
- 4 tbsp greek yoghurt
- 2 cloves garlic, minced
- juice of 1 lemon
- a pinch of salt
- 80g pine nuts
- ½ a 400g can of chickpeas
- 50g butter, melted
- 1 tsp cumin, ground (or paprika)
- a handful of fresh parsley

Breakfast is often overlooked when we think about cuisines from other countries. We would rather celebrate the showstopper at dinner than the simple bowl at sunrise. This recipe does not deviate from one that many Syrians would recognise. It is comforting and delicious, rich and complex, but with only a handful of basic ingredients. A real gem of a breakfast.

Preheat your oven to 200C/400F/gas 6. Chop one of the pitta breads into 2cm squares and toss in the olive oil. Place on a baking tray and toast for 15 minutes until the edges start to brown. With the second piece of pitta bread, rip it into small chunks and lay them in your serving bowls.

In a bowl, add the tahini, yoghurt, garlic, lemon juice and salt, then slowly add 50ml of cold water. The mix will thicken (strangely) and lighten in colour. Add more water if you want it a bit thinner.

In a dry pan on a medium heat, toast the pine nuts until golden brown. Make sure to continually jiggle the pan as burnt pine nuts have a horrible taste. Remove from the pan once toasted and allow to cool.

Drain and rinse the chickpeas and scatter over the ripped pieces of pitta bread, then top with dollops of the tahini yoghurt.

Add the toasted pitta bread on top and garnish with cumin and chopped parsley. Finally, spoon over the melted warm butter and enjoy!

Top Tip: If you have any chickpeas left over from the can then you can roast them with spices of your choice, like paprika or curry powder, for a delicious crunchy snack. Alternatively, you can freeze them in an airtight container.

Photography by @SymmetryBreakfast

Dips & spreads

Small plates

2. MEZZE

"The act of breaking bread is such a strong thing.
If our humble bread can help in any way,
I will be happy."

Fergus Henderson

LABNEH BALLS ROLLED IN SYRIAN HERBS & SPICES V

Donated by Saima Khan
@HampsteadKitchn

"I ate a lot of labneh in the Middle East, and in Syria I saw lots of herbs, spices and nuts being used in the creamy labneh, which was rolled into the prettiest balls."

Serves around 8

2 500g tubs of organic greek yoghurt
2 tsp sea salt flakes
a glug of olive oil to cover

Can be dusted with
dried mint
dried oregano
nigella seeds (baraka seeds)
sesame seeds
smoked paprika
pistachio slivers
smoked almonds, crushed
rose dust and flowers
za'atar

I first discovered these labneh balls in Damascus. I loved the different herbs, seeds and nuts, visually they looked jewel-like. There are so many ways to use these, they taste amazing spread on freshly buttered toast, or instead of sour cream or crème fraîche in a soup. They're so easy to make and versatile, having these prepared ahead of time sitting in the fridge and dusted with herbs just before a dinner party will impress anyone.

Stir the salt thoroughly into the yoghurt.

Put all the yoghurt into a muslin cloth, collect the corners and tie into a bag.

I dangle mine over my kitchen tap and leave a bowl underneath it at room temperature to let the whey strain away. Ideally leave it for at least 12 hours if you can.

Once all the whey has been strained away, you should be left with a thick and creamy mixture.

Spoon into an airtight container and pour over a thin layer of olive oil. It should keep for about 2 weeks.

When you are ready, shape it into little balls and roll in a topping of your choice.

Photography by Saima Khan
Portrait by @KatieWilsonFoto

MOUTABAL (AUBERGINE DIP) V

Donated by Sama Meibar
@Curly_Sama

"I am Syrian but grew up in Cyprus and was lucky enough to have parents who are also amazing cooks. Whilst my mum made the more traditional stews and pastries, my dad made the salads and our dishes for barbecues. In Syria, the food is out of this world – it's rich, full of flavour and plentiful."

Serves 2-4

1 large aubergine
4 tbsp greek yoghurt
2 tsp tahini
1 clove of garlic, crushed
1 squeeze of lemon
olive oil to garnish
pine nuts to garnish
pomegranate seeds (optional)

Moutabal is a traditional part of what I would call a typical Syrian meal. You start with lots of small dishes: moutabal, hummus, olives, halloumi, tabbouleh, fattoush, bread etc. and then move onto the amazing skewers of barbecued marinated lamb or chicken. It's a great mezze and is very versatile.

Preheat the oven to 200C/400F/gas 6.

Wrap the aubergine in aluminium foil and bake in the oven for about 30 minutes. (The alternative here is to slice up the aubergine into discs and deep-fry it until golden brown and tender.)

Take the aubergine out of the oven, peel it, mash it and mix it in with the crushed garlic.

Add the yoghurt, tahini and lemon juice and mix well.

Season to taste, then drizzle with olive oil and use pine nuts to garnish.

If desired, you can mix in pomegranate seeds as well.

Photography by @KatieWilsonFoto
Portrait by @CharlotteHuCo
Styling by @KloellaDeville

MSABACHA (CHICKPEA DIP) V

Donated by Sarit Packer and Itamar Srulovich at Honey & Co.
@HoneyAndCo

Serves 4-6

125g chickpeas
½ tsp bicarbonate of soda
1 tomato, quartered
6 cloves garlic
2 sprigs rosemary
2 sprigs sage
1 tsp cumin seeds
1 tsp salt
1 tsp cumin, ground
50ml olive oil
raw tahini
smoked paprika

For the chilli relish
2 long green chillies
2 cloves garlic
1 lemon
1 tbsp olive oil
a pinch of salt

Traditionally a breakfast dish in the Middle East, but we like to serve our version as a mezze.

Soak the chickpeas overnight in plenty of cold water. In the morning, rinse them off and cover with fresh water, then place in a saucepan and bring to a boil.

Once boiling, add the bicarbonate of soda and skim off all the foam that comes to the top.

Boil for 5 minutes, then strain and re-cover with fresh warm water.

Add the tomato, cut into quarters, then the garlic, rosemary, sage and cumin seeds and cook on a low heat until the chickpeas start to soften (it will take between 40-50 minutes.)

Add the salt, ground cumin and olive oil, then cook for another 10-15 minutes until the chickpeas are melt-in-the-mouth smooth.

Adjust the seasoning if necessary, then remove the stems of the herbs and spoon into bowls. Drizzle with some raw tahini and some of the chilli-garlic relish to taste (see below). A sprinkling of smoky paprika is also nice.

To make the chilli relish, blitz 2 long green chillies (the Turkish type are the best) with 2 cloves of garlic and the flesh from 1 lemon together into a paste, then add 1 tablespoon of olive oil and a pinch of salt.

Photography by @PatriciaNiven

MUHAMMARA (PEPPER & WALNUT DIP) V

Donated by Yotam Ottolenghi and Sami Tamimi at Ottolenghi
@Ottolenghi @Sami_Tamimi

"This is the food which bookends everything we do. The food of Syria is similar to the food of Palestine and Lebanon – the food that we grew up with. There are regional variations, of course, but this food forms a great part of our cooking. Muhammara is a classic Levantine dip made with red peppers, chopped walnuts and spiced with aleppo chilli which you can eat by the spoonful, it's so good. Scoop it up with pitta or it's the perfect addition to a table full of food."

Serves 4 as a dip

- 3 red peppers
- 50g fresh breadcrumbs
- ½ tbsp lemon juice
- 1 tbsp pomegranate molasses
- 1½ tsp ground cumin
- 1 tbsp dried aleppo chilli flakes
- 1 small garlic clove, peeled and crushed
- 50g walnuts, finely chopped by hand
- 2 tbsp olive oil, plus extra to finish
- salt

For the garnish (optional)

- parsley
- mint leaves
- pomegranate seeds

This classic Levantine dip can be made in a food processor, but it will lose some of its lovely texture. I'd use a pestle and mortar if you can. Muhammara keeps well, and even improves after a day in the fridge. Just don't serve it fridge-cold.

Heat the oven to 200C/400F/gas 6. Put the peppers on a tray and roast for 30-35 minutes, turning occasionally, until they are cooked and the skin is blackened. Put the peppers in a bowl, cover with clingfilm and, once cool enough to handle, peel and discard the skin and seeds.

Pat the peppers dry and place in a mortar. Add the breadcrumbs, lemon juice, molasses, cumin, chilli and garlic. Work this with a pestle until well combined, but not so much that the peppers no longer have a noticeable texture.

Stir through the walnuts, a quarter of a teaspoon of salt and the olive oil. Add more pomegranate molasses and salt to taste, you want the flavours to be pretty intense. Spoon the dip into a shallow bowl, using the back of a spoon to give it a wavy texture, and drizzle with a little olive oil. Serve at room temperature.

Optional: Garnish with fresh herbs (such as parsley or mint leaves) and pomegranate seeds

Photography by @PatriciaNiven

PUMPKIN, SPINACH, CHICKPEAS & GOAT'S CURD V

Donated by Jeremy Lee at Quo Vadis
@JeremyLeeQV @QuoVadisSoho

"I would no more assume the knowledge and ability to cook a Syrian dish, bold with great tradition that reaches far back in time, than fly a plane. The inspiration here is freshness, bright flavours and the use of now familiar ingredients such as za'atar."

Serves 4

For the pumpkin

a small grey or orange squash, such as a crown prince or onion squash

a pinch of dried chilli

½ tsp mace

the juice of 1 lemon

3-4 tbsp good olive oil

sea salt

pepper

For the spinach

2 large tbsp olive oil

1 medium-sized potato, peeled and chopped into small pieces

1 small round lettuce

1 small head of celery

3-4 great handfuls of spinach

2 spring onions, or greens of leek, or both

a handful of dill

a handful of coarsely picked parsley

a few leaves of basil

a few leaves of sorrel

nutmeg

For the chickpeas

450g cooked chickpeas

100ml tahini

juice of 1 lemon

1 clove garlic, peeled and chopped

6 tbsp best olive oil

a pinch of ground cumin

pepper

salt

For the goat's curd

200g goat's curd (or ricotta)

4 tbsp olive oil

1 large spoonful mint leaves, chopped

pepper

salt

To finish

feuilles de brick pastry

100g melted butter

salad leaves, various

za'atar

pepper

salt

This lovely recipe has numerous parts, but each is less demanding than the other and makes for a delicious whole that brightens the table splendidly. A nod to the Levant, forever inspiring.

Bake the pumpkin in a moderate oven until it is quite softened and cooked through. Let the pumpkin cool a little before removing the skin and seeds. (It is worth noting that a few pumpkin seeds dried in the oven furnish a pleasing final flourish to this dish.) The flesh should have a gentle density to it, and if requiring a slight further drying then pop it in a pan and cook until all trace of liquid is evaporated. Deposit the pumpkin into a food processor and add the olive oil, the lemon juice and the seasoning and then whizz until smooth. Keep to one side, covered. Do not refrigerate.

For the spinach, gently fry the potatoes for a few minutes, then add enough cold water to just cover. Simmer this with a pinch of salt until the water is almost evaporated and the potato is quite cooked. Pick and wash all the greens thoroughly, then chop coarsely. Drain well in a colander. Add these to the pot and cook well for 5 minutes or so. Liquidise these well until quite smooth, add a scrape or two of nutmeg and then spread out on a tray to cool quickly, stirring often. Remove this to a pan and cover it to prevent it discolouring.

Place all the ingredients for the chickpeas in a food processor and whizz until smooth. Add a little more oil, lemon juice or even water if it is too thick, you want to achieve a soft consistency. Mix all the ingredients for the goat's curd together rather coarsely.

Butter several sheets of feuilles de brick pastry. Season with salt and pepper. Fold them into triangular shapes and bake on a hot sheet in the oven until golden, for around 5 minutes or so. Place on a cooling wire.

To serve, plate up beautiful salad leaves, then some za'atar. Spoon the pumpkin, spinach and chickpea purees into a handsome bowl. Heap on the goat's curd. Tumble some of the salad leaves on and around. Top with a generous dusting of za'atar, then slip the pastry triangles alongside.

Photography by @Joe_Woodhouse

SESAME LABNEH, CHILLI, SUMAC & PRESERVED LEMON V

Donated by Miles Kirby at Caravan Restaurants
@FoodMilesKirby @CaravanRestaurants

Serves 2-4

250g greek yoghurt
50g tahini
3g flaky sea salt
6 large pale green chillies
20ml good white wine vinegar
20g mint leaves, roughly chopped
1 tbsp aleppo chilli
1 tbsp preserved lemon, finely diced
3 tbsp parsley, chopped
50ml olive oil
salt, to taste
pepper, to taste
1 tbsp sumac

We introduced a version of this dish to our menu at Caravan Bankside when we opened in October 2016. We make a rye sourdough flatbread to eat with this dish in the restaurants, but it is equally delicious served with any flatbread. Ideally anything that will soak up all the oily goodness from the plate.

Place a piece of muslin or cheesecloth into a bowl, allowing the fabric to drape over the edges. Pour the greek yoghurt into the cloth, bring the corners together and tie securely with a piece of string.

Hang the cloth for 1½-2 hours. Be sure to position it over a bowl, as it will drip. Once some of the moisture has been squeezed from the yoghurt and it has thickened, remove it from the cloth and place it in a bowl. If you want it thicker, give it a tight squeeze with your hands to release more liquid.

Mix in the tahini and salt and then set aside for later use. If you will not be eating it that same day, then store in the refrigerator until you are ready to use.

Heat a griddle pan until smoking and then char the chillies until they have softened and are marked on the outside with black grill lines. (These are great cooked over coals if you have a barbecue burning.)

Place the cooked chillies in a bowl and pour over the vinegar. Once cool, throw on the chopped mint and set aside.

In a separate bowl, combine the aleppo chilli, preserved lemon, parsley and olive oil. Season to taste and set aside.

To serve, dollop the labneh on to the base of a plate. Using the back of a spoon, spread the labneh unevenly over the base.

Place the green chillies on top of the labneh and then spoon on the aleppo chillies, parsley, and preserved lemon and olive oil mix. Finally, sprinkle over the sumac and serve with your toasted flatbread of choice.

Photography by @PatriciaNiven

SMOKED AUBERGINE & SOUR POTATO FLATBREADS V

Donated by Dean Parker at The Manor
@DeanOParker @TheManorClapham

Makes 24 flatbreads

For the smoked aubergine

4 aubergines, whole
20g smoked butter
20ml arbequina olive oil
3g dried mint
80g yoghurt
zest of 2 lemons
0.5g ground cumin
salt, pepper and lemon juice, to taste

For the flatbreads

150g bread starter (if you have no starter just use 12g baker's yeast)
227g kefir
223g buttermilk (if you have no kefir, use 450g buttermilk)
695g T55 (strong white bread flour)
900g fermented potato (see recipe)
100g golden butter (beurre noisette)

I really love the way that vegetables play a huge part in Syrian and Middle Eastern cuisine, especially aubergines as they are so versatile.

For the smoked aubergine, burn the aubergines really well over a barbecue, or in a dry pan or stove. Leave to cool. Then scrape the pulp out and discard the burnt skin. Blend with the smoked butter, olive oil, mint, cumin, yoghurt and the lemon zest, then season.

To make the fermented potatoes, take 3kg of potatoes, boil, drain and cool, then salt. Leave in a warm (15-20C/60-70F) area for 5 days.

For the flatbreads, take half of the fermented potato and mix with your bread starter, kefir, buttermilk and flour.

Leave the mixture for 8 hours, then refrigerate until cool. Remove from the fridge and roll out flat, then sprinkle the rest of the potato on top. Fold four times, then roll out the dough until 2cm thick. Cut into 24 pieces and place on parchment paper.

Cover your hands in the golden butter and shape the dough as you like.

Leave to prove for 4 hours.

Bake in an oven at 260C/500F/gas 10 for 8 minutes, then barbecue to char slightly.

Serve with the aubergine dip.

Photography by @KatieWilsonFoto

SYRIAN ONION BREAD WITH ROAST BONE MARROW & PARSLEY SALAD

Donated by Fergus Henderson at St. John
@FergusHenderson @St.John.Restaurant

"Having just come back from the Middle East, I was struck by the commonality of the cuisine. The power of the table should bring everyone together."

Serves 4

For the bread
525g self-raising flour
25g sea salt
1½ tsp baking powder
275ml buttermilk
250ml water
olive oil

For the onion and spice topping
50g chopped onions
1 tsp fresh mint, chopped
1 tsp coriander, ground
1 tsp cumin, ground
½ tsp chilli flakes

For the bones
16 pieces veal shin bone, cut to 10cm lengths. (You may have to pre-order these from your friendly butcher. Tell him that you want these bones for marrow.)

For the parsley salad
A healthy bunch of flat-leaf parsley, picked from its stems
2 shallots, peeled and very thinly sliced
1 modest handful of capers (extra-fine if possible)

For the salad dressing
juice of 1 lemon
extra-virgin olive oil
a pinch of sea salt
a pinch of black pepper

For the spiced salt
1 tbsp coarse sea salt
1 tsp sumac

The roast bone marrow has never left the menu at St. John, so it is symbolic of our desire to feed people. And, instead of our usual toasted sourdough, the Syrian onion bread comes in happy rounds to share around the table. The humble act of breaking bread is such a strong thing. It seemed appropriate for this occasion. The bone marrow is also a nod to shawarma, the parsley a nod to tabbouleh and the sumac in the salt gives a sublime citrus backnote.

This bread is extremely forgiving, needing no proving at all. This means that it is best straight out of the oven, but it heats up well too, if you prefer to make it earlier in the day.

To make the bread, sift all the dry ingredients together in a mixing bowl. Create a well in the centre, pour in the buttermilk and water and mix together. Knead the dough until you get a bouncy, smooth, elastic texture.

Divide the dough into two pieces, then roll them into balls on a floured surface and flatten them both into discs. Transfer on to an oiled oven tray, with some space between them, then brush them with more olive oil.

Mix all the ingredients for the topping together and then sprinkle them over the dough. Bake in a very hot oven at 210C/415F/gas 7 for 10 minutes, until the bread is golden in places and the onions have wilted into the spice mixture.

For the marrow, place the bones in an ovenproof frying pan and place in a hot oven, hole-side down. The roasting process should take about 20 minutes, depending on the thickness of the bone. You are looking for the marrow to be loose and giving, but not melting away, which it will do if left too long. (Traditionally the ends would be covered to prevent any seepage, but I like the colouring and crispness at the end.)

Meanwhile, lightly chop your parsley, just enough to discipline it, then mix it with the shallots and capers and, at the last moment, mix and pour over the ingredients for the salad dressing.

Serve the bones on a dish next to a pile of the bread, a pile of parsley salad and a mix of the salt and sumac – this is your spiced salt mix.

A last-minute seasoning, especially in the case of coarse sea salt, gives texture and uplift at the moment of eating. My approach is to scrape the marrow from the bone on to the bread and season with coarse sea salt. Then put a pinch of parsley salad on top of this and eat.

Photography by @KatieWilsonFoto
Portrait by @IssyCroker

ZA'ATAR MIX & FLATBREAD V

Donated by Jack Monroe
@MXJackMonroe

Makes 12 sizeable flatbreads and makes a generous jar or Za'atar

Flatbread

3 cups flour
1 tsp active yeast
1 tsp salt
1 cup milk, preferably full fat

Za'atar

6 tbsp sesame seeds
6 tbsp cumin
6 tbsp fresh thyme, picked
3 tbsp oregano or marjoram
2 tbsp sumac
1 tbsp salt

I was introduced to za'atar by Yotam Ottolenghi, fingering through my well-loved copy of Plenty. Curious, I started to research it, found many a variation and started to put ingredients together. Months later, a good friend of mine, a reverend, invited me for dinner along with a Syrian migrant who was sleeping on her sofa until his Home Office paperwork was completed. As a gift, he had made her a jar of za'atar. It was he who taught me to toast the sesame seeds, and introduced me to another unfamiliar ingredient, sumac. Although there will be countless recipes for za'atar, this one always reminds me of the man with the kind eyes and the humble smile, now reunited with his family, thanks to the kindness of a stranger.

First, gently warm the milk in a small pan on the hob, or on a low setting in the microwave for a minute. Do not let it boil or burn, it should be warm but not hot, or it will kill the yeast. Gently beat the yeast into the milk with a fork, and stand to one side for a few minutes.

Sift the flour into a mixing bowl and add the salt. Make a well, a rough hole, in the centre of the flour. Pour in the milky yeast mixture and mix well to combine into a dough. If it is tacky, and sticks to your hands, then add flour. If it is dry and cracking, add a little oil or water.

Flour your work surface and tip the dough on to it. Knead well for a few minutes, until it starts to feel supple and springy. Cut into equal-sized pieces, set on a baking tray, cover with a cloth, and leave for half an hour to breathe and gently rise.

Preheat your oven to 200C/400C/gas 6. Roll out each flatbread individually, then put them on to a floured baking sheet. Cook for around 12 minutes – you may need to do them in batches. I finish mine on the largest hob on the top of my oven, cautiously passing them through the open flame with a pair of tongs to gently char the edges. Serve with soups, dips, oil and za'atar, split and stuff with leftovers, use as a quick pizza base, or freeze for use in a hurry.

For the za'atar, gently heat a small frying pan and tip in the cumin and sesame seeds. Toast for 30 seconds to a minute, stirring continuously, until the seeds start to brown ever so slightly. You will smell the deep, earthy aroma of the cumin as it starts to release its oils, and then you will know it is time to bring it from the heat.

Tip the warm seeds into a clean, dry jar. I always select the most beautiful jar I can find for this, and display it proudly, a reminder to myself to use it to pep up day-old rice, to stir into yoghurt, to add to soups, to fold into flatbreads.

Pick the thyme and add to the jar, followed by the oregano or marjoram, the sumac and the salt. If your jar is not yet full, continue to add herbs as desired. Tip into a small blender, pulse to combine and give it a good shake to mix. If stored in a cool, dry place with the lid screwed on tight, it can keep for a few months – but mine never lasts so long.

Photography by @PatriciaNiven

FOUL MOUDAMAS V

Donated by Imad Alarnab
@imadssyriankitchen

200g dried fava beans (soaked overnight)
1 handful of parsley
1 tsp cumin
1 tsp salt
3 lemons
3 large tomatoes
3 spring onions

Foul Moudamas is one of the most popular Syrian breakfast dishes. In Damascus, my hometown, having Foul Moudamas on a Friday morning is a ritual. The reasons behind the popularity of this dish are its mouth watering taste, it is cheap and easy to find ingredients and it is also very healthy.

Soak the fava beans overnight and then add to water and simmer for 5 hours on a low heat until very soft.

Once they're ready, drain and add to a large dish.

Mix the cumin, salt, and juice from 3 lemons with the beans.

Chop the parsley, tomatoes and spring onions and add to the dish.

Mix well and finish with a sprinkle of sumac and a drizzle of olive oil.

Photography by @hassanakkad

CHIGA V

Donated by Tomer Amedi at The Palomar
@TomerAmedi @PalomarSoho

"It is important to raise awareness for people who are suffering. #CookForSyria is a way to show that life doesn't always have to be about countries, borders and nations. Sometimes it can just be about people and food."

Serves 4

- 250g fine bulgur wheat
- 2 cups water
- 1 large onion, diced
- 50g tomato paste (about 2 tbsp)
- 2 tomatoes, peeled and chopped
- 3 tbsp pomegranate seeds
- a handful of parsley, chopped
- a handful of mint, chopped
- a handful of spring onion, chopped
- 1 small green chilli, deseeded and finely chopped
- ¾ tsp cumin, toasted and ground
- 5 tbsp olive oil
- 3 tbsp lemon juice
- ½ a lemon, cut into wedges
- 3 tbsp greek yoghurt
- salt
- pepper

This is a great Jewish vegetarian dish coming from a small area named Urfa, on the border of Syria and Turkey. This area has its own unique style of cooking and takes a lot from both regions (you can easily find the resemblance to kibbeh nayyeh – the meaty tartare-like version of it). It's a light dish and makes a great starter or a snack. In this version there is some added yoghurt, which brings creaminess and a bit of sourness to the plate.

Place the bulgur wheat in a bowl and soak for 30 minutes in 2 cups of water. Strain well and press the rest of the water out. Set aside.

Heat a pan to a medium heat and add 2 tbsp of olive oil and the onion. Sauté for 5-7 minutes until golden, then add the tomato paste and sauté for another 3 minutes.

Add the peeled and chopped tomatoes and season with salt, pepper and the cumin. Continue to cook for another 5-7 minutes until the consistency is paste-like, but not too dry, add a bit of water if needed. Set aside to cool, but only for a bit, as it should still be warmish for the next step.

In a bowl, mix the cooked paste, bulgur wheat, herbs, chilli, 2 tablespoons of the pomegranate seeds, 2 tablespoons of olive oil and the lemon juice. Season with salt and pepper.

Once the mixture is even and tasty, shape with the aid of 2 wet tablespoons so that they become rounded, oval-like patties.

To serve, make a small well with the yoghurt on each plate. Place the patties on top and garnish with the rest of the pomegranate seeds, the olive oil and the wedges of lemon.

Photography by @KatieWilsonFoto

RAW SALMON KIBBEH WITH YOGHURT FLATBREAD

Donated by Bruno Loubet at Grain Store
@Bruno_Loubet @GrainStoreKX

"At Grain Store, there are no geographical boundaries to our menu, so I love to explore flavours from all around the world. I am quite familiar with and passionate about the cooking from this part of the world. There is a huge cross-over of dishes and recipes between countries."

Serves 4

400g salmon fillets
2 tbsp shallots, finely chopped
½ tsp harissa
¼ lemon, zest and juice
½ tsp ground cumin
1 tbsp fresh coriander, finely chopped
2 tbsp natural yoghurt
2 tbsp olive oil
2 tbsp pomegranate seeds
olive oil, to drizzle
sumac
pepper
salt

For the flatbread
200g plain white flour
2 tbsp olive oil
4 pinches of salt
100g water
1 sachet dried yeast (7g)
1 drop orange blossom water
½ tsp sugar

The Syrian touch in this dish is definitely the spice element. This dish is traditionally made with lamb, but I thought it would work perfectly with salmon. Kibbeh is sometimes fried but there is also a raw version. It's kind of like a Middle Eastern tartare.

The night before, season the salmon on the flesh side with salt and pepper and the grated lemon zest. Place in the fridge for 12 hours for a light curing.

In a mixing bowl, place the yeast with the water and sugar. Whisk well to dissolve, then add two tablespoons of flour and whisk again to break up any lumps.

Cover with a cloth and place in a warm area until it doubles in volume, then add the remaining ingredients for the flatbread.

Work the dough with the hook on a mixing machine for a good 5 minutes, or until shiny and elastic. Cover with a cloth and place in the fridge for at least 2 hours.

Dice the salmon into small chunks. Place in a bowl with the remaining ingredients, except for the pomegranate, and mix well.

Take the flatbread dough out of the mixing bowl and place on a work surface. Work it with the palm of your hand for a couple of minutes, then place it in a bowl. Cover with a cloth and rest for 10 minutes in the fridge.

Take out and cut into 4 even pieces. Shape into 4 balls. With the top of your fingers, stretch the dough to a round, thin disk like a pizza. Then cook it on a hot barbecue for a minute on both sides.

For the garnish, combine the yoghurt, olive oil, salt and pepper. Divide the salmon kibbeh between the plates, then sprinkle with the pomegranate seeds, sumac and a dollop of the yoghurt sauce. Drizzle some good olive oil over the top and serve with the flatbread.

Photography by @PatriciaNiven

SYRIAN BEEF TARTARE

Donated by Nuno Mendes at Chiltern Firehouse
@NunoViajante

"I have always been fascinated by Syrian food and knew a fair amount already. It is one of the oldest cuisines in the world, full of unique flavours from Persia to Palestine and beyond."

Serves 2 to share

For the tartare
140g high-quality steak mince
½ a shallot, chopped
6g preserved lemon
aleppo pepper flakes, ground
15g extra-virgin olive oil
1g sumac
2 splashes orange blossom water
2 splashes rosewater
maldon sea salt

For the freekeh
200g boiled freekeh, cooled and seasoned
5 splashes orange blossom water
5 splashes rosewater
30g extra-virgin olive oil
a large pinch of dried mint
orange zest
lemon juice
a pinch of cumin

For the tartare garnishes
5g freekeh
5g preserved lemon
a dollop of hung yoghurt with sumac
olive oil
4g green pistachios, toasted
2g rose petals, dried
pistachio oil
1g aleppo pepper flakes
a sprig of mint
warm flatbread

For the hot sauce
100g apples, chopped and peeled
60g onions
3 cloves garlic
60g red chillies
40ml red wine vinegar
40ml water
25g sugar
80g tomatoes, grated
0.5g mint, dried
1 splash rosewater
1 splash orange blossom water
1 pinch sumac
1 small pinch cumin
6g rose petals
100ml olive oil

In Syria and the Middle East there is a mezze dish called kibbeh nayyeh, which is made with raw meat and various spices. We have taken the Chiltern Firehouse steak tartare and seasoned the meat with flavours common in Syrian cooking such as preserved lemons, pistachios, rosewater, orange blossom, freekeh and pulses. We're serving it with warm Syrian flatbread and a hot sauce. I am so excited by this dish, I was so inspired by the flavours of Syria and where it took this dish – I love it.

For the tartare, combine all of the ingredients in a bowl. Mix well, cover and chill.

Combine all of the ingredients for the freekeh in a separate bowl and mix well.

The hot sauce ingredients will make a decent amount, any additional sauce can be kept refrigerated in an airtight container for future use.

To make the hot sauce, smoke the apples, garlic, onion and chillies for 2 hours. Then cook down in a large pan with the vinegar, water and sugar until the mixture turns a dark colour – this should take around 1 hour on a low heat.

Blitz, pass and chill overnight. The next day, correct the consistency and re-season if necessary.

To this mix, add grated tomatoes, dried mint, the rosewater and orange blossom water, sumac and cumin. Cook the mix down for 1 hour at a low temperature. Finish with 6g of rose petals and 100ml of olive oil.

On a plate, add the tartare and the freekeh in even-sized mounds, then arrange the garnishes neatly around those mounds and finish with a spoonful of hot sauce. Serve with warm flatbread on the side.

Photography by @KatieWilsonFoto

CONFIT DUCK KIBBEH WITH SMOKED AUBERGINE LABNEH

Donated by Joel Braham at The Good Egg
@TheGoodEgg_

"We were amazed and excited to learn how diverse Syrian cooking is, and the richness of the Syrian Jewish tradition. We've eaten lots of similar dishes before from the Levantine region, but it's the little things that make those dishes Syrian that were the most interesting to find out. Our favourites from all the research were the manoushi flatbreads and makdous, stuffed, pickled baby aubergines."

Serves 4

For the confit duck
2 duck legs (gressingham)
1 tbsp maldon sea salt
1 red chilli
1 green chilli
1 red onion
4 cloves garlic, peeled
1 tsp black peppercorns
1 tsp coriander seeds
1 cinnamon stick
2 cloves
1 tsp cumin seeds
2 cardamom pods
500ml rapeseed oil or duck fat

For the kibbeh dough
400g soaked coarse bulgur wheat (approximately 200g dry)
75g white onion, diced
1 tsp sesame seeds
1 tsp cumin, ground
1 tsp maldon sea salt
100g confit duck

For the kibbeh filling
100g dried apricots soaked in honey and hot water
150g confit duck
5g allspice
20g pine nuts, toasted
100g date syrup

For the aubergine labneh
2 large aubergines
300g labneh (or thick greek yoghurt)
2 cloves garlic
salt
black and white sesame seeds

We love kibbeh, which are found all over the Middle East, and researching lots of different Syrian versions inspired us to do our own take on it. Our twist comes with swapping the traditional ground lamb for our baharat-spiced duck awarma. The process of making awarma makes the duck super tender, and gives the filling a softer, more unctuous texture. Awarma is like a rich Middle Eastern confit, and is the perfect base for a sweet duck kibbeh. The sweetness of the date syrup and dried apricot brings two familiar Middle Eastern flavours to the table and works really well with the duck.

First, cure the duck legs by rubbing with the sea salt and leaving to rest in an ovenproof dish. Leave uncovered in the fridge for 2 hours or overnight. Preheat the oven to 120C/250F/gas ½ and add all the other confit ingredients to the dish. Pour over the oil/fat and then seal tightly with tin foil.

Cook for 2.5 hours. After that it should be soft enough to easily pull the meat apart with a spoon and a fork. If it needs longer, put it back in at 140C/275F/gas 1 for another 30-40 minutes. When it is done, take it out and leave it to cool to room temperature in the oil/fat. Then remove the legs, chillies and garlic cloves. Place in a bowl and using two forks, shred the meat, garlic and chillies, removing the bones at the same time.

Using the naked flame of your gas hob, or under a gas/electric grill, burn the aubergines until they are black and charred all over. Allow to cool, then peel and add the smoky flesh to a food processor along with the labneh, garlic cloves and a good pinch of salt. Pulse until combined and set aside. Take 100g of the pulled duck mixture and place in a food processor along with the rest of the kibbeh dough ingredients. Blitz until you get a smooth dough. Refrigerate while you prepare the filling. With the 150g of duck in your bowl, roughly chop the soaked apricots and add all the rest of the ingredients into the mix, combining well along with a little seasoning to taste.

Take your kibbeh dough and roll into roughly 30g balls, putting them on a lined oven tray. Then, take a dough ball and make a well in it with your thumb. Push a heaped teaspoon of filling into the hole and using your hands, smooth the dough over the filling. Work into a mini dome shape, pinching the top to make a pointy spire, and put back on the tray.

When they are all filled and shaped, sprinkle with black and white sesame seeds and deep-fry in batches of 4 or 5 until they are a rich dark brown in colour, which should take around 2 minutes. You can either use a deep-fat fryer set to 180C/355F, or heat the oil in a large saucepan on the hob.

Remove the cooked kibbeh and place on a tray lined with kitchen paper to drain, then serve while still warm on a smear of the burnt aubergine labneh.

Photography by @KatieWilsonFoto

FALAFEL WITH WINTER SLAW & YOGHURT V

Donated by Tom Hunt at Poco Tapas
@TomsFeast @PocoTapasBar

"I discovered that Syrian falafel are often made into a small doughnut shape like I have done in this recipe. This helps the falafel cook more evenly and throughout the middle. A Syrian friend also told me that the hole in the middle makes a good carrier for tahini."

Slaw serves 4
Falafel mix makes 16-20 balls

For the slaw

1 satsuma, peeled and pulled into segments

2 sticks celery, roughly sliced including leaves

100g brussels sprouts, finely sliced

½ red onion, finely sliced

3 sprigs mint, leaves picked, stalks finely chopped

3 sprigs parsley, leaves picked, stalks finely chopped

100g pickled turnips (optional)

For the falafel

200g dried chickpeas, soaked for 8 hours or more (preferably overnight)

½ small onion, peeled and roughly chopped

1 clove garlic, roughly chopped

20g coriander, stalks and leaves roughly chopped

1 tsp cumin, toasted

1 tsp baking powder

1 tsp salt

1½ tbsp flour (optional)

oil for frying

yoghurt, chilli sauce and flatbread to serve

I'm a huge fan of all the different varieties of falafel. Every country in the Middle East has its own way of making this dish. In Syria they usually make falafel with chickpeas, whereas in Egypt they use fava beans, but both can also be used in combination. A Syrian-style falafel is often made with an abundance of coriander and parsley. For this recipe, I've created a sharp, wintery slaw to accompany the comforting falafel balls.

Drain the chickpeas, allow them to dry a little and then put them into a blender with all the other falafel ingredients except the oil. Blend for a minute into a rough paste.

Decant into a bowl and roll into small 1-inch patties. Pierce a hole through the middle with a skewer or the reverse end of a fork and place on a tray in the fridge.

To prepare the slaw, combine all of its ingredients and put to one side.

Fill a medium high-sided saucepan with about an inch of oil. The pan should be less than a third full to allow for the oil to rise when frying.

Put on a medium heat. If you have a thermometer then bring the heat to 180C/350F. If not, then put a small amount of the mixture into the oil. When it floats to the top and bubbles a lot then the oil should be hot enough to fry.

Fry the falafel in batches of 6-7 at a time so that the oil doesn't drop too much in temperature. Turn them after a minute or two. When the falafel are nutty and brown, remove them from the fat with a slotted spoon and place in a warmed bowl.

Serve with the slaw, flatbread, and yoghurt.

Photography by @KatieWilsonFoto
Styling by @KloellaDeville

POTATO KOFTE V

Donated by Itab Azzam and Dina Mousawi of Syria Recipes From Home
@ItabAzzam @DMousawi @Syria_RecipesFromHome

"I discovered that there is a lot of Syrian cuisines similar to Iraqi cuisine. There's some difference but a lot of similarities. The potato koftes are one of my favourite Syrian dishes, we have a similar thing in Iraq." - Dina

Makes approximately 14 individual pieces

350g mashed potato
25g breadcrumbs
salt and pepper to taste
vegetable oil for frying

For the stuffing
1 medium onion, finely diced
40g parsley, finely chopped
2 tbs sultanas
2tbs pine nuts
2tbs pomegranate molasses
salt and pepper, to taste

These delicious little mashed potato balls will be popular with anyone at a supper club. You can make them in advance and then fry them at the last minute. You could also add minced meat to the stuffing if you prefer. We made these in Beirut while researching our book. We cooked with a group of Syrian women who taught us many of their special recipes and this was one of them. As meat can often be expensive they make these vegetarian options instead.

You can use left over mash for this recipe. If you're making it fresh, Lady Balfour's work well and you need 475g of unpeeled potatoes. Peel, and boil the potatoes, trying not to over boil them; then drain very well. Mash the boiled potatoes, season and leave to cool.

On a low heat, caramelise the onions then add the pine nuts and sultanas and cook for a couple of minutes longer. Turn the heat off and immediately add the finely chopped parsley.

Add the breadcrumbs to the mashed potatoes and mix well with your hands.

Take a small amount of potato and make into a ball roughly the size of a ping-pong ball. Flatten it out in the palm of your hand, put about a teaspoon of the stuffing in, be careful not to overfill, then close and make into little round flat shapes, you can smooth out any cracks with a tiny bit of water.

Once you have made all the potato kofta, heat some oil in a non stick pan; add the kofta and fry for 2-3mins on each side or until they turn golden brown.

Serve immediately with a salad or as part of a mezze.

Photography by @KatieWilsonFoto
Styling by @KloellaDeville
With thanks to Backgrounds Prop Hire

SABUDANA VADA, MUHAMMARA, SESAME RAITA & CORIANDER CHUTNEY V

Donated by Will Bowlby at Kricket
@KricketLondon

"Once you start exploring the origins of Indian cuisine you'll quickly see the footprint of Syrian and Middle-eastern flavours and ingredients running throughout."

Serves 4

For the sabudana vada

250g sabudana (tapioca) pearls

4 medium potatoes, cooked and mashed

125g crushed roasted peanuts

a handful of chopped coriander

1 red onion, finely chopped

1in piece of ginger, finely chopped

10 fresh curry leaves, finely sliced

a squeeze of lime

salt and sugar to taste

1 tsp roasted cumin seeds

3 green chillies, finely chopped

For the muhammara

4 red peppers, roasted, de-skinned and deseeded

2 cloves of garlic, minced

1 tsp kashmiri chilli powder

125g roasted walnuts

a squeeze of lime

125ml extra-virgin olive oil

50g fresh breadcrumbs

For the sesame raita

250g full-fat greek yoghurt

100g tahini paste

2 cloves garlic, minced

salt and sugar to taste

For the coriander chutney

3 bunches coriander

2 cloves garlic

1in piece of ginger, peeled

2 green chillies

lemon juice, salt and sugar to taste

1 tsp oil

I wanted to choose a dish with a humble background – what better than an Indian street food classic. The key Syrian element in it is the muhammara, which is a hot pepper dish originally from Aleppo.

Soak the sabudana pearls for at least 5 hours, preferably overnight, in cold water. Once drained, mix all the ingredients for the vada together and form small patties. Set aside in the fridge until needed.

For the chutney, roughly chop the coriander and place in a blender, then add all the other chutney ingredients apart from the oil and blend until a rough paste is formed. Slowly add the oil to create a smooth consistency. Season with salt, sugar and lemon juice. If you want to make this chutney ahead of time, omit the seasonings until the last minute, as left too long, they will start to discolour the chutney.

For the muhammara, combine all the ingredients in a blender and blend to a rough paste. This can be done in a pestle and mortar for a more rustic finish.

For the sesame raita, combine all the ingredients together in a bowl and mix thoroughly.

Heat vegetable oil in a large deep pan until the temperature reaches approximately 180C/356F. When the oil is hot enough, add the sabudana patties and cook until golden brown.

Drain on kitchen paper and serve immediately with the sesame raita, muhammara and coriander chutney.

Photography by @TuckAndVine

ZA'ATAR-SPICED FALAFEL WITH ROASTED CHICKPEA & PARSLEY HUMMUS V

Donated by Ella Mills
@DeliciouslyElla

"Food should be a way of bringing people together – I love meals where everyone shares lots of different dishes, so I'm a big fan of the 'mezze'-style eating that is common in the Middle East."

Makes 16 falafel

For the hummus
2 tins chickpeas
1 tsp paprika
a drizzle of olive oil
1 lemon, juiced
salt
pepper
1 heaped tbsp tahini
1 clove garlic
a few sprigs of parsley
180ml olive oil
80ml water

For the falafel
2 tins chickpeas
salt
pepper
2 tbsp za'atar
2 cloves garlic
2 tbsp tahini
3 tbsp chickpea (gram) flour
3 tbsp olive oil
1 lemon, juiced

Falafel and hummus are my all-time favourites and are so adaptable – you can have lots of fun playing with flavour combinations to make a few basic ingredients taste really special! I haven't done much cooking with za'atar in the past so enjoyed experimenting with it to give my dishes some Syrian flavour.

To make the hummus, preheat the oven to 200C/400F/gas 6. Drain and rinse the chickpeas and pat them dry with kitchen roll. Place them in a baking tray and sprinkle over the paprika, salt and a drizzle of olive oil. Bake in the oven for 20 minutes, then remove and leave to cool.

When the chickpeas are cool, peel and roughly chop the garlic, then blend with all the ingredients in a food processor until smooth.

For the falafel, preheat the oven to 220C/425F/gas 7. Drain and rinse the chickpeas and peel and crush the garlic, then add all the ingredients to a food processor and pulse a few times until a chunky mix forms. Line a baking tray with greaseproof paper.

Taking a spoonful of falafel mix at a time, roll it into balls in your hands and place on to the tray, then bake the falafel balls for 40 minutes, turning them over halfway through cooking. Serve with lots of your roasted chickpea and parsley hummus!

Photography by @KatieWilsonFoto
Portrait by @Sophia_Spring_Photography
Styling by @KloellaDeville

SYRIAN DUMPLINGS WITH SMOKED AUBERGINE, YOGHURT, ZA'ATAR & DILL V

Donated by Skye Gyngell at Spring
@SkyeGyngell @Spring_Ldn

"I was really excited when we were given the opportunity to create a dish for #CookForSyria – it's always nice to be given a challenge to come up with something different. I love the flavours of the Middle East – they are vibrant, clean, clear and strong, so although it is very different to the way we cook at Spring it also seemed like a very natural fit."

Makes between 10-12 dumplings

For the dough

- 30g sourdough starter
- 300g 00 flour
- a pinch of salt
- between 200-400ml water
- roughly 500ml vegetable oil, for deep frying
- za'atar, to garnish

For the filling

- 2 shallots, peeled
- 2 garlic cloves, peeled
- 1 bunch swiss chard, washed
- 1 aubergine
- 50g freekeh
- dry chilli flakes
- zest and juice of 1 lemon
- salt

For the yoghurt sauce

- 250ml yoghurt
- ½ clove garlic, grated
- 3 sprigs mint, chopped
- a small bunch of chives, chopped
- 3 sprigs dill, chopped
- juice of ½ a lemon

For the tomato and pine-nut salsa

- 3 green tomatoes
- 20g pine nuts
- 1 red chilli, chopped
- a small bunch of flat-leaf parsley, chopped
- 50ml good-quality olive oil
- 25ml red-wine vinegar

I didn't know a lot about Syrian cooking so I read up a little on the culinary history of Syria – it's very similar in feel to much of the food from the Levant. Dor, who is an Israeli chef here at Spring, and I discussed what might be nice – and the dumplings came from there.

For the dumplings, combine all of the dry dough ingredients together, then add water slowly. Knead the dough until it is smooth and springs back. (You may not need all the water, if you think the dough is too wet, add some flour and keep kneading.) Rest for a minimum of 2 hours, preferably overnight.

For the filling, boil the freekeh in water until cooked, strain and put to one side. Meanwhile, prick the aubergine with a small knife and place on the stove on an open flame until softened and the skin has a good char. (You could also cook under the grill in your oven.) When cooked, remove the green top and some of the skin. Reserve some skin for an extra-deep charred flavour. You may need to place it on a strainer to remove any excess liquid.

Chop the chard finely. Cook in boiling water for a minute, then strain and place on kitchen towel to absorb any extra liquid.

Chop your garlic and shallots finely and cook in olive oil with some dry chilli until very soft. Combine the chard, aubergine, freekeh and the onion mix together, and then season with salt, lemon zest, dry chilli and lemon juice.

Once the dough is ready, roll it to about 2 millimetres in thickness. If using a pasta machine, roll to the 2 setting twice. When you've reached the desired thickness, cut the pastry into large squares. Place a tablespoon of filling in the centre, then fold one corner to the furthest corner from it, creating a triangle.

Press around the filling firmly and use a knife to cut the edges, creating a wonton-shaped dumpling. Place on a tray lined with baking parchment.

To make the tomato salsa, toast the pine nuts slightly. Then quarter the tomatoes, discard the seeds and dice roughly. Combine the chilli, tomatoes, parsley, pine nuts, oil and vinegar and season with salt.

To assemble the dish, first warm the vegetable oil for deep frying. (Make sure it's not too hot by dipping a small piece of bread in before.)

Place 3 dumplings at a time in the oil. Meanwhile, combine all ingredients for the yoghurt sauce. Fry the dumplings until golden brown, then remove, drain on kitchen towel and sprinkle with za'atar. Place the dumplings on a plate, layering yoghurt sauce between each dumpling. Finish with tomato salsa.

Photography by @KatieWilsonFoto
Portrait by @Amber_Rowlands

YALANGI V

Donated by Rosy Rong, pictured, and Tommy Tannock at The Store
@RosyRong @TheStoreKitchen

"Cooking is a powerful way to find a connection with people, and so often the most exciting things happen when cultural traditions migrate and meet. What better way to spread this message than by bringing people together to enjoy a meal."

Serves 4

- 1 spanish onion, finely diced
- 2 cloves garlic, finely diced
- 4 very ripe vine tomatoes
- ½ tsp allspice
- 3 lemons, juiced
- olive oil
- fine sea salt
- 400g brown rice
- parsley, finely chopped
- 3 bunches of chard, with the stems removed from the leaves, the leaves gently steamed for 30 seconds and ⅓ of the stems finely diced

We hosted the launch dinner for the #CookForSyria campaign here at The Store, 180 The Strand. We designed this dish as a canapé. People are familiar with dolmades, but we wanted to give them a fresh feel. Stuffed vine leaves are eaten across most of the Middle East.

We wanted to source our ingredients locally, and were excited to read on Anissa Helou's fantastic blog that Swiss chard leaves are sometimes used. In Syria, the vegetarian versions are called yalangi, which is Turkish for "fake".

To cook the rice, first rinse it in plenty of cold water. Put twice the amount of water as rice into a pot on a high heat. Cover and bring to the boil. Check the rice every 5 minutes to make sure that there is enough liquid. Once it is almost cooked, remove the lid and make sure that all of the excess liquid cooks off. Never drain your rice or you'll lose all the flavour!

Fry the allspice off in a glug of olive oil, and add the onion and sweat until soft and nicely coloured (about 10 minutes). Add the chard stems with a pinch of salt and cook on a medium heat for about 20 minutes, until the mixture has browned and combined nicely.

Now turn the heat up, add more salt and oil and add the tomatoes and garlic, stirring continuously. Once the tomatoes start to lose their water, you can turn down to a simmer and let the mix reduce. Make sure to cook it until thick, with sauce-like consistency before adding the rice.

Combine the warm rice with the sauce, then add the finely chopped parsley and lemon juice. Season to taste. Remember that once cool, flavours are duller, so you can be generous with the salt. Spread the rice out in a pan or a baking sheet to cool it down quickly, and put it away in a sealed container. Give your rice mix a little time in the fridge for the flavours to mature.

While the rice is in the fridge, steam your chard leaves for a minute, just until they soften and are pliable. Pat the excess liquid away and lay the leaves out flat.

Take a chard leaf (you can cut them into halves or thirds if the leaf is big) and put on one dollop of the cold rice mix. Roll the leaf forward, tucking in the sides as you go. Store these in the fridge while you are rolling the others (never leave the rice out of the fridge).

Lightly roast the stuffed leaves in the oven at 180C/350F/gas 4 for a few minutes on each side, and then store in a container of olive oil. They should last for up to 5 days. Don't forget to enjoy your handiwork!

Photography by @KatieWilsonFoto
With thanks to @TommyTannock & @JohnnieCollins

YAPRAK (DOLMADES)

Donated by Sophie Michell
@SophieMichell

Makes 16-20 dolmades

100g basmati rice
200g jar of vine leaves in brine, drained
100ml extra-virgin olive oil
200g minced lamb
2 garlic cloves, crushed
1 onion, finely chopped
50g sultanas
50g pine nuts
1 tsp ground cinnamon
1 tsp dried oregano
1 tbsp tomato puree
a small handful of flat-leaf parsley, freshly chopped
1 lemon, juiced
greek yoghurt or labneh

To serve
black pepper, freshly ground
salt

Dolmades can be found all over Greece, Turkey, Syria and Lebanon. I have tested so many recipes, and this comes out as my favourite every time. I like the addition of lamb and the sweetness of the sultanas. Homemade dolmades served slightly warm with a touch of yoghurt really make a lovely dish – and are a world away from the ready-made ones that you find in delis and shops.

Cook the rice according to the packet instructions. Drain if necessary and set aside. Soak the vine leaves in boiling water for 5 minutes, then drain and set aside to cool.

Place a large frying pan over a medium heat and pour in half the olive oil, add the lamb, garlic and onion and fry for about 10 minutes until the mixture starts to turn golden. Add the sultanas, pine nuts, cinnamon and oregano and fry for a further 5 minutes.

Finally, add 50ml of cold water and the tomato puree, stir well and cook for 5 minutes.

Stir in the cooked rice and the parsley, season well and set aside to cool.

Preheat the oven to 160C/325F/gas 3.

Place 1 vine leaf on a chopping board with the veins facing up, then spoon 1 dessertspoon of filling on to the centre of the leaf. Carefully fold in the sides of the leaf and tightly roll it up – the trick is not to add too much filling. Place the stuffed leaf into a 15 x 20cm ovenproof dish. Repeat using the remaining filling, packing the stuffed leaves tightly together in the dish.

Mix the remaining oil with 50ml of hot water and the lemon juice. Pour over the vine leaves, season, cover with foil and bake for 1 hour.

Serve the dolmades warm with a big dollop of yoghurt or labneh on the side. They are also great served chilled as a snack or starter.

Photography by @PatriciaNiven

3. SALADS & VEGETABLES

"I have always loved the flavours of this part of the world. Imagine what we could do if all of us did one little thing to help."

Thomasina Miers

CRISPY KALE & ROAST SQUASH MUJADARA V

Donated by Rosie Birkett
@RosieFoodie

The humanitarian crisis that is happening in Syria is completely devastating, and it's easy to feel totally helpless. Being a little part of a big movement, and encouraging people to mobilise – not just locally but globally – through the universal act of cooking and eating means that in some small way I can try to help. I'm very proud to be supporting this campaign.

Serves 2-4
(depending on greed)

½ tbsp rapeseed oil
100g kale, with the thick stems removed and the leaves torn into crisp-sized pieces
1 tbsp sumac
1 tsp red chilli flakes
1 tbsp white sesame seeds
½ tsp sea salt
1 butternut squash, peeled with the seeds removed and cut into wedges
2 tbsp olive oil
1 tbsp thyme leaves
1 tbsp runny honey
salt
pepper
2 white onions, finely sliced
160g puy or green lentils
1 bay leaf
160g long-grain or basmati rice
1 tbsp olive oil
juice of 2 lemons
1 tsp cumin seeds
1 tbsp fresh coriander
1 tsp ground cumin
1 tbsp tahini
6 tbsp natural yoghurt

This dish is inspired by mujadara – a Syrian and Middle Eastern staple with many regional variations, based around lentils and rice or bulgar. Mine has a British twist.

Soak the lentils for half an hour in cold water before you cook them. Preheat the oven to 150C/300F/gas 2.

Toss the kale lightly in the rapeseed oil, salt, sesame seeds, chilli and sumac, massaging the leaves until coated with the oil and seasoning. Arrange the leaves in one layer over roasting trays or baking tins – you might need to use more than one to keep them in an even layer. Roast in the oven for 15-20 minutes, until crisp and dry but not brown.

Once dried, remove from the oven and turn the heat up to 180C/350F/gas 4. Toss the butternut squash in 1 tablespoon of olive oil with the thyme leaves, honey, salt and pepper and arrange in a single layer on a roasting tray. Roast for 30-40 minutes, until tender.

Heat 1 tablespoon of olive oil in a non-stick frying pan and add the sliced onions and a pinch of salt. Cook for 10-12 minutes, until softened and caramelising.

Cook the rice and lentils in two separate pans at the same time. Cook the lentils in a litre of water with a bay leaf and a pinch of salt. Bring to the boil, then reduce the heat, cover with a lid and simmer for 15-20 minutes, until they are puffed and tender, but still holding their shape.

Rinse the rice under cold water and then place in a pan with double the quantity of water. Bring to the boil, then turn the heat right down. Cover the pan with a lid and leave, untouched, for 15 minutes, after which the moisture will have been absorbed. Place the rice into a large bowl and fluff the grains with a fork. Stir the lentils through with the onions, lemon juice and olive oil. Season to taste.

Heat 1 tablespoon of olive oil in a non-stick frying pan. Add the cumin seeds and cook for a couple of minutes, until they crackle, then add the ground cumin and stir. Remove from the heat.

In a bowl, stir the natural yoghurt and tahini together until smooth. Pour in the cumin oil and stir.

Spread the lentil and rice mix out on to a sharing platter. Top with the butternut squash, fresh coriander and kale chips. Serve with the cumin-spiked yoghurt.

Photography by @KatieWilsonFoto
Styling by @KloellaDeville

FOUL MOUKALA (SAUTÉED BROAD BEANS WITH GARLIC AND CORIANDER) V

Donated by Dalia Dogmoch Soubra
@DaliasKitchen

Serves 6

1kg broad beans
70ml olive oil
6-8 garlic cloves, minced
100g fresh coriander, finely chopped
¼ tsp salt
juice of 1 lemon
250g yoghurt
pitta bread

This dish, the name of which means sautéed beans in Arabic, is particularly Syrian when the broad beans are young and small in size, which makes them tender as their skin is not chewy. When the smaller kind, which are common in Syria, cannot be found then the beans must be podded and their skin removed. This makes for a more flavoursome dish. It is served as a side dish or a cold "mezze" starter with yoghurt, lemon and bread on the side.

In a large pot, bring enough water to a boil to cover the broad beans. Drop them gently in the water and simmer for 5 minutes.

Drain the beans and drop them in ice water. Pierce the skins with a small sharp knife or using your finger, and push the beans out. Discard the skins.

In a pan, warm the olive oil on a low heat, being careful not to burn it. Add the garlic and coriander and cook for a minute without browning, just to release the flavour.

Drop the podded beans into the pan with the salt, remove from the heat and stir to gently combine everything.

Add the lemon juice, stir and serve at room temperature or cold with bread and yoghurt.

Photography by @SukainaRajabali

1/3 CUP

GREEN FREEKEH SALAD WITH SMOKED ALMONDS & POMEGRANATE SEEDS V

Donated by Saima Khan
@HampsteadKitchn

"Having travelled and worked extensively all across the US, Europe, Middle East and Asia, what I enjoyed the most was the sharing of food. .The Middle East has a fantastic food sharing culture. The tradition of sharing a meal is an essential part of spending quality time with the family - one should never eat alone, I certainly never did."

Serves 6

- 500g freekeh (buy online or from any Middle Eastern store)
- 1 bunch flat-leaf parsley
- ½ bunch fresh mint, chopped
- ½ bunch dill
- 1 bunch spring onions, finely chopped
- 1 can chickpeas, drained and tossed in a pan with smoked cumin and paprika
- juice of ½ a lemon, more to taste if you prefer
- 1 pinch cumin seeds, toasted and ground
- 1 garlic clove, minced or pureed (optional)
- a pinch of sea salt
- 6 tbsp extra-virgin olive oil
- a scattering of pumpkin seeds
- 1 pomegranate, deseeded
- a handful of smoked almonds, coarsely cut

Freekeh is very versatile, and having made 100kg of this once at the Calais camps, it is very dear to me, and it reminds a lot of the Syrian refugees of home. I add whatever I have in the fridge, you can add roasted vegetables, black olives and any kind of nut or herbs, mine keeps evolving to whatever we have in our kitchen.

Heat a medium-sized heavy saucepan over a medium heat and add the freekeh. Toast in the dry pan, shaking or stirring for 2-3 minutes until the freekeh becomes fragrant.

Add the freekeh to a pan of boiling water, the grain should be whole but soft when pressed with your fingers. Boil for around 15-20 minutes.

Drain the freekeh and run under a cold tap to stop it cooking and becoming mushy.

In a large bowl, combine the freekeh with the chopped herbs, spring onions and chickpeas, then toss together.

In another bowl, lightly whisk together lemon juice, cumin, garlic, salt and olive oil, then toss with the salad.

Scatter the pomegranate seeds, almonds and pumpkins seeds on the top, then give it one last toss and it's ready.

Serve right away or let sit for up to 1 hour. It will keep for 3 or 4 days in the fridge.

Can be served with roast chicken, lamb or fresh bread, or simply on its own as a salad.

Photography by @KatieWilsonFoto

PICKLED AUBERGINES, SALT, LEMON & CHILLI V

Tom Harris and John Rotheram at The Marksman
@Marksman_Pub

"It was important for us to be able to integrate the dish for this campaign into our menu and into the style of food that we cook, so after some research into Syrian cuisine, a pickled dish stood out. Most guests at The Marksman start their meal with pickles, so we feel that this will be a popular choice."

Serves 4

For the brined aubergines
4 aubergines
1 litre water
30g salt

For the devilled dressing
100g deseeded chillies, grilled
2 wedges salt lemon
40g capers
2g saffron
50ml olive oil

For the pickle
100ml white wine vinegar
60g caster sugar
30ml water
a pinch of sumac
parsley, chopped

What was really interesting when we started our research into Syrian food was to find out how similar it is to Turkish cuisine, which is one of our favourites to eat when we are out. The Syrian element of our dish is the method of pickling the aubergines, which are in themselves a staple ingredient in Syrian cuisine.

For the brined aubergines, peel and slice the aubergines into thin strips. Place in a large sealed container and add the other brine ingredients. Leave at room temperature for 2 days.

For the devilled dressing, chop the chillies, salt lemon and capers into a fine paste using a knife, not a food processor, otherwise it will emulsify the paste and make it too creamy. Once all the ingredients are finely chopped, incorporate the olive oil and the saffron.

Drain the brined aubergines, then blanche quickly in boiling water and leave to drain in a colander for about an hour to make sure that all the excess water is removed.

Combine the aubergines with the devilled dressing in a mixing bowl then incorporate all the pickle ingredients.

Serve in a small dish and garnish with a pinch of sumac and chopped parsley.

Works well with bread served on the side.

Photography by @KatieWilsonFoto
Styling by @KloellaDeville

ROAST MINI POTATO SALAD WITH WALNUT SAUCE & POMEGRANATES V

Donated by Thomasina Miers at Wahaca
@ThomasinaMiers @Wahaca

I knew quite a bit about Middle Eastern food anyway, as I grew up in Shepherd's Bush, and have always loved the flavours of this part of the world. I think the research made me think deeper about the country and where certain dishes and ingredients first came from. Aleppo chilli flakes are one of the ingredients I use most at home – appalling to think now of the state that famous city is in...it made the horror of the war even more tangible.

Serves 6-8 as a starter

- 1kg baby potatoes
- 3 sage leaves
- 4 tbsp olive oil
- a large pinch of sea salt, flaked

For the walnut sauce

- 1 large garlic clove, crushed
- 150g walnuts
- 50g slice of sourdough bread
- 200ml olive oil
- 200ml water
- 1 tsp sea salt, flaked
- a pinch of ground cinnamon

To finish

- good quality sherry vinegar
- good quality extra-virgin olive oil
- 2 heads of red chicory, cut into slithers, or a large handful of watercress
- 1 large pomegranate
- aleppo chilli flakes

I was inspired by Mexico's national dish, chiles en nogada, which uses walnuts and pomegranates. When I heard about the book I started thinking about the dish and its origins. Mexico had a large Lebanese population, which would have had some influence, but Aztecs and Mixtecs had been grinding nuts and seeds for hundreds of years to enrich and add protein to simple dishes of wild leaves, vegetables, beans and tortillas. Syria's cuisine didn't feel too dissimilar in the way that it uses nuts extensively in its recipes, not to mention pomegranates and spices. Its tendency to stuff vegetables with braised meats, which came to Syria via Persia, also resonated.

For the salad that I created, instead of stuffing a Mexican chilli pepper I decided to make the walnut sauce a central part of the recipe, more as a Syrian-style mezze, a dip for the roast potatoes. The original dish and my adaptation contain pomegranate seeds, an ingredient prized in both countries. In place of the poblano chile that the Mexican dish calls for I use aleppo chilli flakes for a scattering of heat to season the other flavours.

Heat the oven to 200C/400F/gas 6. Toss the potatoes in the sage, oil and sea salt in a roasting tin and roast for 30-40 minutes, or until golden, crisp and tender.

Roll the pomegranate firmly across the work surface to release the seeds. Cut it open over a bowl to catch the juices. Use another bowl to discard the white, bitter pith. Tear the fruit open into 3 or 4 pieces and tease out the seeds into the juice bowl, picking out any pith.

Meanwhile, blitz the crushed garlic and walnuts together in a food processor until you have a very fine crumb and the mix starts to smell strongly of walnuts. Blitz again with the bread, salt and cinnamon and slowly incorporate the water and oil, until you have the consistency of hummus. It will thicken as it stands so if serving later, you may want to loosen it again with a little more water or oil. Taste again and season if necessary.

Make a pool of the sauce on each plate, then top with 3 or 4 potatoes and drizzle over half a teaspoon to a teaspoon of sherry vinegar and olive oil. Top with the leaves, pomegranate seeds and a dusting of chilli flakes. Season with a touch of salt and serve.

Photography by @KatieWilsonFoto

ROASTED ROOTS WITH CANDIED SESAME & TAHINI YOGHURT V

Donated by Nicholas Balfe at Salon Brixton
@NicholasBalfe @Salon_Brixton

"There's a number of Syrian/Middle Eastern dishes and methods that I've discovered through my research that I'm really looking forward to incorporating into my menus. I really like to use fruit in savoury dishes, which is definitely inspired by cooking from that region..."

Serves 4 as a starter or a side

a dozen or so heritage carrots, cleaned but not peeled (multicoloured ones are great, but any that are bunched and still with their tops on will do)

olive oil

a bunch of thyme

a few cloves of garlic, crushed

sea salt

black pepper

dried chilli (aleppo pepper/turkish chilli flakes have a brighter, fruitier flavour)

a pinch of sumac

For the yoghurt

250g thick greek yoghurt

1 small clove garlic, crushed, grated or very finely chopped to a paste

2 tsps tahini

the juice of ½ a lemon

a pinch of sea salt

For the candied sesame

100g sesame seeds

100g caster sugar

sea salt

a splash of water

The dish is a summation of some of the Middle Eastern flavours that I'm into (sesame/tahini, sumac, warm spices) melded with a simple preparation of a very humble seasonal ingredient – the carrot! The seasoned yoghurt is a very important part of the dish, not just a garnish for the carrot, but a key component in its own right, adding acidity and a velvety texture, as it would be used in Syrian cooking. Sesame/tahini is also present in lots of Syrian dishes, although I've candied them for extra crunch and to make the flavour pop! Finally, aleppo pepper, with it's fruity, warm heat, rather than fiery spice, adds a unique Syrian character. (If you can't find aleppo pepper, then turkish chilli or dried chilli will do.)

Preheat the oven to 180C/350F/gas 4. Pick off some of the greenest, perkiest carrot tops and rinse well. Reserve for the garnish. Toss the carrots in olive oil and salt, and roast in the oven with the thyme and the garlic until tender and beginning to caramelise. This should take around 20 minutes, depending on the size of the carrots.

To make the candied sesame, prepare a heatproof tray with a nonstick baking mat or a sheet of baking paper laid out inside it. Heat a large frying pan or a skillet over a medium heat. Sprinkle the sugar over the surface and add just enough water for it to become sandy.

Sprinkle over the sea salt and leave to cook and then caramelise. If it looks like it's cooking unevenly, you can shake the pan, but don't stir it as it can crystallise the caramel. Keep cooking until it becomes a golden caramel colour. Add the sesame seeds, stir a couple of times to combine, and pour out onto the nonstick mat/baking paper. Be careful as it'll be very hot.

When it's cool and the caramel is hard, bash it up in a pestle and mortar, or pulse in a food processor to form a crumb. Now make the yoghurt mixture by combining the yoghurt, tahini, garlic and lemon. Taste as you go and add the quantities of each that you like.

By now, the carrots will be ready. Remove from the oven and toss with chilli and sumac. Serve a few on each plate with a blob of yoghurt, a sprinkle of candied sesame crumbs and a few carrot tops.

Photography by @TuckAndVine

GLAZED SQUASH WITH ROSEHIP HARISSA & TAHINI V

Donated Doug McMaster and Matt Stone at Silo Brighton
@SiloBrighton

"I wanted this dish to be something that people can easily replicate and to reach the widest target audience using ingredients that both incorporated the Silo zero-waste mentality and Syrian flavours."

Serves 2

1 small squash (300-400g), cut into thirds, seeds removed
280g sesame seeds
6-8 tbsp rapeseed oil
sumac
citric acid
linseeds, toasted
500g rosehip
a drop of cooking oil
1 tbsp fermented chilli
1 clove garlic
oil
salt
edible flowers, such as marigolds or nasturtiums, to garnish

During the research for this dish I was able to discover how the real taste of some of Syrian foods can be as we were able to get some fresh sumac, which had such a vibrant flavour. It was important to keep this dish vegetarian, in the end it turned out to be vegan. The Syrian elements are the harissa and sumac tahini. The tahini alone was bitter, but the sumac provided the ideal solution and it was satisfying using a traditional Syrian ingredient that we were able to source locally.

Cut the squash into thirds, then remove the seeds and season with salt and a small drop of oil. Heat the oven to 180C/350F/gas 4 and cook the squash for 12 minutes, then allow it to cool slightly before removing its skin.

For the tahini, toast the sesame seeds and then blend with enough oil to make a tahini consistency. The mixture will need a decent amount of salt to be mixed in, but it is very important not to add any more liquids (hence the use of citric acid rather than lemon juice) as liquid will simply react with the oil and make it form a dense paste.

Add as much salt, acid and sumac as you need to turn the tahini from a bitter mix to a well-balanced and delicious sauce. Use the tahini to glaze the squash over a wire rack, in order to avoid spillage on the plate.

Toast the linseed, or flaxseeds, in a pan. Apply to the squash once it has been glazed. (This adds a little texture to the dish.)

For the harissa, mix the rosehip, chilli and oil in a ratio of roughly 3:2. The oil just serves the purpose of letting the harissa loosen a little. Only a small amount of garlic is required for this dish, it shouldn't be overly noticeable.

Add all the elements of the dish to a plate and garnish with edible flowers such as marigolds or nasturtiums; red or orange ones would work particularly well.

Photography by @CharlotteHuCo

SYRIAN FATTOUSH SALAD V

Donated by Marianna Leivaditaki at Morito
@MoritoTapas

"Being involved with #CookForSyria means a lot to us. Having been inspired by Syria's cuisine for a long time this is a project focused on the young people that presently need help, and we all should contribute to the best of our ability."

Serves 6 as a sharing dish

25g butter, melted
1 large flatbread (about 20cm in diameter)
1 aubergine, diced and lightly salted
10 ripe cherry tomatoes, cut into quarters
1 watermelon radish, diced
1 small bunch of radishes, cut into quarters
1 cucumber, diced
½ a small cauliflower, cut into tiny florets
1 handful wild rocket leaves
1 handful fresh mint, shredded
1 handful flat-leaf parsley, shredded
½ tsp za'atar
vegetable oil, for frying the aubergine

For the dressing
6 tbsp extra-virgin olive oil
1 tbsp pomegranate molasses
1 tbsp lemon juice
2 tbsp pomegranate juice, freshly squeezed
1 tsp sumac
1 tsp za'atar
a pinch of sugar
salt, to taste

In Morito Hackney Road we are serving a winter fattoush which is so beautiful to look at and full of amazing winter vegetables like watermelon radishes, cauliflower and purple carrots. We make a fresh pomegranate juice dressing enriched with pomegranate molasses to create a fresh, sweet and zesty flavour. We sprinkle lots of za'atar and sumac over the top which give it a lovely aromatic herbal depth. For the Syrian fattoush we add some sweet tomatoes, fried aubergine and pomegranate seeds, a combination of flavours from Syria that make it even more delicious and a pleasure to eat.

Preheat the oven to 180C/350F/gas 4. Brush the melted butter on to the flatbread and bake in the oven for 10-15 minutes until golden and crispy. Remove from the oven and set aside to cool.

Heat some vegetable oil in a small saucepan and fry the aubergine until golden brown. Remove from the pan using a slotted spoon and transfer to a plate lined with kitchen paper to absorb any excess oil.

Make the dressing by placing all of the ingredients in a jam jar and shaking really well. Put all of the vegetables and herbs in a bowl and pour over the dressing.

Lightly crush the flatbread into the bowl, mix everything together, then check the seasoning and serve immediately.

Photography by @PatriciaNiven

SYRIAN-INSPIRED ENSALADA SIERRA V

Donated by Martin Morales at Ceviche and Andina Restaurants
@MartinMoralesCeviche @CevicheUk @AndinaLondon

"Syrian recipes are rich in tradition and stories and reflect the rich culture of a people from many origins and roots; akin to Peru."

Serves 4

150g quinoa

100g broad beans, skinned and cooked

a small handful coriander leaves, chopped

1 aji limo, or yellow scotch-bonnet chilli, deseeded and finely chopped

1 ripe avocado, stoned, peeled and sliced very thinly on the diagonal

To serve

1 small red onion, finely chopped

2 small tomatoes, deseeded and finely chopped

pomegranate seeds (optional)

For the dressing

20 physalis fruits, with the husks discarded

2 tbsp granulated sugar

1 aji limo, or 1 medium red chilli, deseeded and finely chopped

4 tsp extra-virgin olive oil

Quinoa is a great substitute for bulgar wheat and when creating any quinoa-heavy salads, we have always looked at the original tabbouleh for inspiration. So our ensalada sierra takes from that, with its pomegranate, quinoa, andean uchucuta herb sauce and broad beans it brings the Syrian mountains and the Peruvian Andes together with harmonious flavours.

Wash the quinoa in cold water until it starts to run clear. Put in a saucepan, cover with cold water and add a pinch of salt. Bring to the boil and simmer for 15–20 minutes until the quinoa is well cooked and the grain has started to unfurl. Drain, cool and set aside until needed.

To make the sauce, put the physalis and sugar in a saucepan and add enough water to half-cover the contents. Cook slowly over a low heat for 10-15 minutes until the water has reduced by two-thirds and the physalis are soft. Remove from the heat and leave to cool. Transfer to a small food processor or blender and blitz until smooth.

Next, make the dressing by adding the physalis mix to the other dressing ingredients. Put all of the ingredients in a bowl and mix together well. Add the broad beans, coriander and chilli to the quinoa and mix well. Add 3 tablespoons of the dressing, making sure that you don't oversoak the quinoa mixture.

To assemble the salad, put a deep, 12-15cm ring mould on a plate (or use a large cookie cutter). Arrange the avocado in the bottom of the mould and, using the back of a spoon, press down firmly. Fill the rest of the mould with the quinoa and broad bean mix, and press down well again. Drizzle 2 tablespoons of the physalis sauce around the edge, then remove the mould.

Finally, mix together the onion and tomato and put 2 tablespoons of this on top of the quinoa. Alternatively, simply tumble the salad on to a plate. Add pomegrantates to garnish and pour over more dressing if you feel that it is needed.

Photography by @CharlotteHuCo

WARM PITTA, YOGHURT & CHICKPEA SALAD V

Donated by Elly Curshen

@EllyPear

Serves 4

- 3 large pitta breads
- 1 can chickpeas
- 200g greek yoghurt
- 1½ tbsp tahini
- juice of ½ lemon
- 1 clove garlic, crushed or finely grated
- 1 tsp cumin
- 3 tsp olive oil

To garnish

- 1 tsp olive oil
- 2 tbsp pine nuts
- a big pinch of smoked paprika
- a big pinch of sumac
- a small bunch of mint, leaves picked and left whole
- 25g feta
- 3 radishes, very finely sliced
- a drizzle of argan oil or good extra-virgin olive oil
- a small handful of pickled turnips or beetroot, cut into bite-sized pieces
- smoked maldon sea salt
- black pepper, freshly ground

All over the world, you'll find variations of this idea – dry (stale or toasted) bread, given new life by soaking it in liquid. Panzanella in Italy, bread pudding in England, strata in the US. This warm vegetarian salad is my version of a fattet hummus – a Middle Eastern savoury chickpea bread pudding. It is eaten as a brunch dish all over the region, is very easy to make and is absolutely packed full of protein so it's great for veggies. It is creamy, nutty and comforting. I've gone to town with the toppings, as is my way, but feel free to play around. Getting a good contrast between the creamy base layer and some toasted bread, crunchy radishes or pickles is, however, essential – it's what makes every mouthful special.

Preheat the oven to 180C/350F/gas 4. Put the pitta breads on a baking tray, drizzle both sides with olive oil and put them into the oven for 10 minutes.

Tip the chickpeas and their liquid (reserving 3 tablespoons) into a saucepan to warm through. Add the cumin and 2 teaspoons of olive oil. Stir well over a medium heat, bring to a simmer and then reduce the heat to low to keep warm while you make the rest of the salad.

Put the yoghurt into a large mixing bowl, add the tahini, lemon juice, garlic and the reserved liquid from the chickpea tin and whisk well.

Fill a medium-sized saucepan with 2cm of water, sit your mixing bowl on top and over a medium heat so that the water is just simmering, gently heat the yoghurt mixture. Whisk regularly so the mixture is just warmed through and the flavours are blended together. This will take about 5 minutes.

Cut the baked pitta breads into 1-inch squares and separate the two layers. Reserve a handful for garnish and spread the remaining bread out on the platter. Drizzle a couple of ladlefuls of the warm chickpea cooking broth over the bread until they are just soaked.

Strain the chickpeas and layer them on top of the soaked bread. Spoon the warmed yoghurt mixture over the chickpeas and gently fold the layers together.

Heat 1 teaspoon of olive oil in a frying pan, add the pine nuts and fry until they are starting to turn golden. Keep a close eye on them as they will burn very easily.

Scoop the pine nuts out of the frying pan and put to one side, add the reserved bread to the frying pan with a splash more oil and toast until golden and extra crispy.

Spoon the pine nuts over the surface of the platter, crumble over the feta, scatter the mint on top, add the radish slices, the crispy bread, smoked paprika, sumac, drizzle the whole lot with some argan oil, add pickled turnips and season with the smoked salt and pepper.

Photography by @KatieWilsonFoto
Portrait by @MylesNew
Styling by @KloellaDeville

WINTER FATTOUSH WITH STICKY TAMARIND BEEF, ROASTED PEARS, CAVOLO NERO, BITTER LEAVES & CRISPY BREAD

Donated by Selin Kiazim at Oklava

@SelinKiazim @Oklava_Ldn

"Through my research into Syrian cuisine, I discovered just how alike it is to Turkish cuisine – I love all of those Middle Eastern flavours, the food is incredibly fresh and vibrant."

Serves 4

2 short ribs

1 block tamarind

50g dark brown sugar

30ml sherry vinegar

2 tbsp unsalted butter

2 william's pears, cut in half, cores removed

1 lemon, juiced

2 cloves garlic, finely grated

2 tbsp sumac

100ml extra-virgin olive oil

1/2 loaf bread – I like to use the baharat bread we make at the restaurant.

1/2 bunch parsley washed and roughly chopped

80g cavolo nero, washed, stalks stripped and chopped

1/2 cucumber, washed, cut in half lengthways and de-seeded

8 breakfast radishes, finely sliced and placed in iced water

4 spring onions, finely sliced on the angle

1/4 head radicchio, roughly chopped

4 tbsp mint

4 tbsp thick yoghurt

4 tbsp pistachios, crushed and toasted

fine salt, to taste

maldon salt, to taste

Fattoush has to be one of my favourite salads so I jumped at the chance of creating a funky version encompassing Syrian and Turkish flavours (which are all so similar). I adapted my recipe by using spices like the baharat mix and sumac. Also, incorporating tamarind into the recipe, which I didn't realise was an ingredient which is used quite a bit in Syrian cooking.

Preheat the oven to 180C/350F/gas 4. Season the short ribs with fine salt, place into a roasting tray and cook for 2-3 hours. Pick the meat off the bone into large chunks once cool enough to handle.

To make the tamarind glaze, place the tamarind in a small pot and cover with just enough water. Gently simmer for 20 minutes, then pass through a fine sieve. Add in the brown sugar and sherry vinegar.

Put the butter in a large frying pan, gently melt and add in the pears, cut side down. Place in the oven for 10 minutes or until golden brown and cooked through. Allow to cool. Tear into large chunks. Turn the oven down to 150C/300F/gas 2.

To make the sumac dressing, combine the juice of 1 lemon, 1 grated garlic clove and 1 tbsp sumac. Whisk together, while gently drizzling in 50ml olive oil. Season. Break the bread up into chunks, place onto a baking tray and place in the oven to dry out. This should take around 10-15mins.

To make the parsley oil, mince the bunch of chopped parsley leaves with 1 clove of minced garlic and 50ml olive oil.

Bring a large pan of water up to the boil. Add in the cavolo nero and boil for 3-4 minutes. Drain and allow to cool. Dress with a little maldon salt and olive oil whilst warm.

In a large frying pan, add in the short ribs at a medium-high heat, add in 4-5 tbsp of tamarind glaze and toss around to form a sticky coating on the beef. Take out of the pan and season with maldon salt.

Slice the cucumber into 1cm slices.

To assemble the salad, mix together in a large bowl the cucumber, cavolo nero, radish, spring onion, raddichio, chicory, 4 tablespoons of parsley leaves, mint leaves, crispy bread and pears. Season with maldon salt and sumac dressing to your liking.

Place a dollop of yoghurt on the plate; place the pile of salad to one side. Scatter over some pieces of short rib, drizzle around the parsley oil, sprinkle a little sumac and the pistachios.

Photography by @KatieWilsonFoto

4. SOUPS & STEWS

"For those, like me, who live to eat, it's pretty mind-bending to think of how many people in the world still eat to live."

Yotam Ottolenghi

AUBERGINE & CHICKPEA STEW V

Donated by Ella Mills
@DeliciouslyElla

"I love cooking simple food that is easy to make and can be enjoyed by everyone."

Serves 4

2 aubergines
6 cloves garlic
1 tsp cinnamon
1 tsp paprika
1 tsp cumin
2 tsp za'atar
salt
pepper
a glug of olive oil
1 red onion
4 tomatoes, chopped
2 tbsp tomato puree
1 tin chopped tomatoes
1 tin chickpeas
3 tsp apple-cider vinegar
coconut yoghurt
chopped coriander

Chickpeas and aubergines are the Syrian element to my recipes. They are such an underrated and amazingly versatile ingredients, so I wanted to show a few different ways of cooking with them. Stews are my winter staple, they are so lovely and warming!

Preheat the oven to 200C/400F/gas 6. Chop the aubergine into large chunks and place in a baking tray. Sprinkle with the salt and pepper, paprika, cumin, za'atar and cinnamon. Add in 4 garlic cloves and drizzle everything with a good glug of olive oil. Roast for 25 minutes.

While they cook, finely chop the red onion and add it to a pan with a drizzle of olive oil. Cook this on a low heat for 10 minutes, until the onions are cooked through, then add in the remaining garlic, tomatoes, tomato puree and tinned tomatoes, bring to the boil and let simmer for 20 minutes.

Finally add the aubergine, chickpeas, salt and apple-cider vinegar, cooking for another few minutes until the chickpeas are warmed through.

Serve your stew with a dollop of coconut yoghurt and a sprinkling of chopped coriander.

Photography by @KatieWilsonFoto
Portrait by @Sophia_Spring_Photography
Styling by @KloellaDeville

BLACK-EYED BEANS WITH CHARD & GREEN HERB SMASH V

Donated by Anna Jones
@We_Are_Food

"There is a sense of sharing that food brings, an intuitive and tactile way of communicating, of sharing our humanity. As a mother and a human, I want every child on this planet to be safe and fed and #CookForSyria is a joyous step in that direction."

Serves 4

For the beans

1 leek

1 tbsp coconut oil or olive oil

2 cloves garlic

a good pinch of chilli powder, or dried chilli, chopped

2 × 400ml tins of black-eyed beans

1 tsp vegetable stock powder, or ½ a stock cube

a good grating of nutmeg

½ an unwaxed lemon

200g bunch of swiss or rainbow chard

For the herb smash

a large bunch of fresh coriander

2 green chillies

2 cloves garlic

30g walnuts, shelled

1 tbsp runny honey, or maple syrup

2 tbsp good olive oil

juice of ½ a lemon

This dish is not a classic Syrian recipe, but one that takes inspiration from the classic and simple Syrian bean stews. The beans are cooked simply and in keeping with tradition with tomatoes, chilli and spices – cinnamon and nutmeg both used in Syrian kitchens. The finished stew is freshened up with a herb and walnut smash, using verdant green herbs and walnuts to make an amazing flavour packed green herb smash to spoon over and crown the finished stew.

Fill and boil a kettle and get all of your ingredients together. Put a large saucepan on the heat. Wash and finely slice the leek. Add to the saucepan with a tablespoon of coconut or olive oil and cook for a couple of minutes until soft and sweet.

Finely slice the garlic and add to the pan with the chilli powder or dried chilli and cook for a couple of minutes, until the garlic is beginning to brown. Add the black-eyed beans with their liquid, the stock powder or cube and the passata and bring to a simmer.

Grate in the nutmeg, squeeze in the juice of half the lemon, add the squeezed lemon half to the pan and simmer for 10 minutes or topping up with a little hot water from the kettle as needed. Meanwhile, strip the leaves from the chard stalks. Finely slice the stalks and add them to the pan, then finely shred the leaves and put to one side.

Put all the ingredients for the herb smash into a food processor, squeeze in the juice of the other half of the lemon and blitz until you have a smooth, grassy paste. Season well with salt and pepper.

Once the black beans are soft and flavourful and the liquid has reduced to a thick, soup-like consistency, stir in the chard leaves, season well with salt and pepper and leave to cook for a couple of minutes. Scoop into deep bowls and spoon over the herb smash. If you're really hungry, some rice or flatbread would go well with the dish.

Photography by @KatieWilsonFoto

FREEKEH CHICKEN

Donated by John Gregory-Smith
@JohnGS

"I have been cooking Syrian food for years, it's incredible. The cuisine is so varied, with a wonderful variety of fresh, vibrant dishes. The food culture is old and has influenced many other parts of the Levantine."

Serves 4

For the dough

2 tbsp olive oil

1kg chicken thighs, on the bone with the skin left on

1 onion, finely chopped

200g lamb, minced

200g freekeh

4in cinnamon stick

4 cardamom pods

2 tsp baharat

1 tsp ground black pepper

600ml chicken stock

20g almonds, flaked

30g pine nuts

200g greek yoghurt

2 tsp mint, dried

juice of ½ a lemon

60g pomegranate seeds

a small handful of mint leaves, roughly chopped

a small handful of parsley leaves, roughly chopped

sea salt

This is a traditional dish, using simple spices like baharat or seven spice, cinnamon and cardamom. Normally the whole chicken is poached and shredded. I have used chicken thighs and cooked everything together to speed things up. The nuts are a classic garnish. I have gone a bit fancy and added fresh herbs and pomegranate seeds, as well as a dry mint yoghurt, which really works with the freekeh. It's so simple, hearty and delicious and I know that once people taste it, they love it.

Heat the oil in a large non-stick pan over a medium heat. Add the chicken and brown for about 5-6 minutes each side. Remove from the pan and set to one side.

Reheat the pan over a high heat. Add the onion and lamb mince and stir-fry for 4-5 minutes, or until wonderfully golden. Tip in the freekeh and add the cinnamon, cardamom, baharat, black pepper and a good pinch of salt. Mix well so that all of the spices coat the grains of freekeh.

Pour in the stock and bring to the boil over a high heat. Nestle the chicken pieces into the freekeh. Cover, reduce the heat to low and cook for around 45 minutes-1 hour, or until all the stock has been absorbed and the freekeh is tender. It should be moist but not wet. Check the seasoning and add more salt if needed. If the freekeh is too wet, continue to cook for 5-10 minutes without the lid.

Meanwhile, chuck the almonds and pine nuts into a small non-stick pan and heat over a medium heat. Toast for 3-4 minutes, shaking the pan occasionally, or until a little golden. Remove the pan from the heat and leave to cool.

Scoop the yoghurt into a mixing bowl and add the dried mint, lemon juice and a good pinch of salt. Mix together and transfer to a serving bowl.

To serve, spoon the freekeh into a large serving dish and arrange the chicken over the top. Scatter over the nuts, pomegranate seeds and fresh herbs. Serve immediately with the yoghurt.

Photography by @Joe_Woodhouse

HARAK OSBAO (LENTILS & PASTA WITH TAMARIND, SUMAC & POMEGRANATE)

Donated by Yotam Ottolenghi and Sami Tamimi at Ottolenghi
@Ottolenghi @Sami_Tamimi

"We're cooking a dish called harak osbao which directly translates to mean 'he burnt his finger' – a reference to it being so irresistible that you can't help but get stuck in. It's a mix of lentils and pasta with lots of flavour injected in with the tamarind water, chicken stock and pomegranate molasses in which it's cooked. Fresh herbs, sharp sumac, refreshing pomegranate seeds – it's beautiful comfort-food fit for a feast."

Serves 8-10

- 40g tamarind, soaked in 200ml boiling water
- 250g fettuccini, broken up roughly
- 60ml olive oil
- 2 red onions, thinly sliced (around 350g)
- 350g brown lentils
- 1.5 litres chicken stock
- 2 tbsp pomegranate molasses
- 6 garlic cloves, crushed
- 30g coriander, roughly chopped
- 20g parsley, roughly chopped
- 90g pomegranate seeds
- 2 tsp sumac
- 2 lemons, cut into wedges
- flaky sea salt
- black pepper

This is a dish for a feast, but it is extremely comforting and delicious with all the toppings mixed in.

Mix the tamarind with the water well to separate the pips. Strain the liquid into a small bowl, discarding the pips, and set aside.

Place a large saucepan on a medium-high heat and once hot, add the broken-up fettucini. Toast for 1-2 minutes until the pasta starts to brown, then remove from the pan and set aside.

Pour 2 tablespoons of oil into the pan and return to a medium-high heat. Add the onion and fry for 8 minutes, stirring frequently until golden and soft. Remove from the pan and set aside.

Add the chicken stock to the pan and place on a high heat. Once boiling, add the lentils, reduce the heat to medium and cook for 20 minutes or until soft.

Add the toasted fettucine, tamarind water, 150ml water, pomegranate molasses, 4 teaspoons of salt and lots of pepper.

Continue to cook for 8-9 minutes until the pasta is soft and almost all of the liquid has been absorbed and set aside for 10 minutes. The liquid will continue to be absorbed, but the lentils and pasta should remain moist.

Place a small saucepan on a medium-high heat with 2 tablespoons of oil. Add the garlic and fry for 1-2 minutes, until just golden brown. Remove from the heat and stir in the coriander.

Spoon the lentils and pasta into a large, shallow serving bowl. Top with the garlic and coriander, parsley, pomegranate seeds and sumac, and serve with the lemon wedges.

Photography by @PatriciaNiven

MAUDA STEW

Donated by Eyal Jagermann at The Barbary
@EyalJ @BarbaryLondon

"For us at The Barbary, Syrian cuisine is linked to our culinary heritage, particularly the naan e barbari, and is part of the menu every day. I think #CookForSyria is a significant project with a very important cause, and we are happy to contribute and help in this small way."

Serves 4

8-10 chicken drumsticks/ thighs

500g potatoes, peeled and cut into chunks

1 big white onion, peeled and finely chopped

4 cloves of garlic, finely chopped

1 chilli, seeds removed and finely chopped

a handful of flat parsley, chopped

For the baharat spice mix

2 tbsp black peppercorns

1 cardamom pod

1 tsp cinnamon

A classic dish from the Halabi kitchen that symbolises the beauty in the simplicity of Syrian and indeed Middle Eastern cuisine. It is a dish that is both easy to make at home and lovely to share, especially in this autumnal cold weather. The Syrian elements in the dish are the unique flavours from the baharat spice mix, which is very traditional in the cuisine, but also the philosophy of people eating together and sharing a big pot of delicious stew. It is a social event and a great way to enjoy a meal.

To make the spice mix, add all the spices to a pestle and mortar and crush together. In a heavy pot, heat up 3 tablespoons of olive oil.

Season the chicken well with salt and the baharat mix, then sear in the pot on all sides so that they are golden brown. Take out the chicken and set aside. In the same pot, add the potatoes and brown on all sides.

When the potatoes are brown, add the onion, garlic and chilli with a bit more salt and the baharat mix, then stir for a few minutes.

Put the chicken back into the pot and mix everything together. Cook for 10 minutes until the onion and garlic are caramelised.

Add water to the pot to cover ¾ of the stew. Bring to the boil, reduce to a low heat and cook covered for 40 minutes.

Take off the lid and cook for 10 more minutes, then check the seasoning. Sprinkle with chopped parsley and good olive oil.

To be served with plain basmati rice, creamy tahini sauce and fresh fattoush salad. Enjoy!

Photography by @KatieWilsonFoto

SAJJEYYA (BEEF STEW WITH ARAK)

Donated by Itab Azzam and Dina Mousawi of Syria Recipes From Home
@ItabAzzam @DMousawi @Syria_RecipesFromHome

"I think the beef stew is my mum's favourite, and I just saw her recently in Lebanon and she reminded me, so I said I'll make it for this."

Serves 4

500g Beef cubes
100g beef fat minced
2 aubergines, cubed
2 green peppers
2 small onions, sliced
300g cherry tomatoes (cut in half)
125ml of Arak or Ouzo
salt and pepper, to taste

This is a dish from Southern Syria. Arak which is a type of alcoholic drink very similar to Ouzu is made mainly in that region. This is a dish usually made to accompany a barbecue. In the summer friends and families would go to the mountains for a picnic and cook it on an open fire in a pot called Saj, and that is where this dish name come form.

Cover the beef in water and boil for 45 minutes, meanwhile cut all the vegetables.

Take the beef out of its water and in another large pan, fry the beef fat for a couple of minutes before adding the beef along with the vegetables.

Add few spoons of the water left from boiling the beef.

Cover and leave to simmer for 25 minutes. Then add the Arak and simmer for a further 5 minutes.

Serve with flat bread or rice.

Photography by @KatieWilsonFoto
Styling by @KloellaDeville
With thanks to Backgrounds Prop Hire

MUSHROOM BROTH, SMOKED GREEN WHEAT FREEKEH & ZA'ATAR V

Donated by James Walters at Arabica Bar and Kitchen
@ArabicaBarAndKitchen

"I was inspired to create this dish by cold autumnal forest walks."

Serves 2-3

25g dried porcini mushrooms
1 litre warm water
45g freekeh
80ml olive oil
1 large banana shallot
2 cloves garlic
½ stick cinnamon
¾ tsp za'atar
10g enoki mushrooms
½ lemon
½ tbsp flat-leaf parsley
sea salt, to taste
black pepper, to taste

Freekeh (smoked green wheat) is one of my favourite Middle Eastern store cupboard ingredients. The wheat is harvested while young and green, sundried and then set on fire, giving it an earthy, lightly smoky flavour that works wonders with the rich, intense earthiness of the dried porcini and adds texture and bite to offset against the mushrooms in the broth.

Za'atar is a quintessential Middle Eastern spice blend of wild thyme, sumac (a sharp, citrusy berry) and toasted sesame. Addictive with warm bread and olive oil, commonly enjoyed sprinkled onto creamy, thick strained yoghurt for breakfast or as a salad seasoning. I've added a generous teaspoon into the mix to pull out the thyme and sesame notes, using the citrusy tang of the sumac to help cut through the richness of the dried porcini-based broth.

Place the dried porcini mushrooms in a small bowl, cover with the warm water and leave them to soak for 45 minutes.

Sort through the freekeh and remove any grit or debris, then leave it to soak for 30 minutes under running water, removing any debris that floats to the top, before draining.

Peel and finely dice the shallot and garlic.

Warm 70ml of olive oil in a large, deep saucepan, add the shallots and cook them over a medium heat for 10 minutes until they soften and turn a pale, golden colour, then add the garlic, cinnamon and za'atar and cook for a further 2 minutes.

Add the freekeh, the porcini mushrooms and their water to the pan and bring to the boil, reduce the heat, cover and gently simmer for 30 minutes. The freekeh is cooked when it's fluffed up but retains a slightly chewy texture.

Remove the lid, add the enoki mushrooms, lemon juice and the finely chopped parsley.

Season the soup with salt and pepper and ladle it into deep bowls, then drizzle with the remaining 10ml of olive oil.

Photography by @PatriciaNiven

Lemon zest, pinenuts

HOUSE PICKLES

Cucumber, cauliflower, peppers, carrot, turnip, chilli

- **SPICED LAMB**, onion, pine nuts, sumac
- **SPINACH** onions, pine nuts, sumac

#COOKFORSYRIA CAMPAIGN

PORCINI MUSHROOM BROTH

Smoked green wheat freeke, Za'atar

#CookForSyria is a month-long celebratic cuisine and awareness for the great crisis of our generation. ***£2 from*** *towards the Unicef Children*

HUMMUS

Chickpeas,

HUMMUS

Toaste

ROAS

Tat

CLAY OVEN

FETA & SPINACH BOREGI

dill, crisp buttery

SHEH

NAGE WITH PUMPKIN & BARBERRY DUMPLINGS V

Donated by Olia Hercules
@OliaHercules

"I have been in love with Syrian food from my early teens."

Serves 4 hungry people

For the nage (vegetable broth)
- 2 carrots, scrubbed and roughly chopped
- 1 bulb fennel, roughly chopped
- ½ a celeriac, peeled and chopped
- 2 sticks celery, roughly chopped
- 2 shallots, halved
- 1 bay leaf
- a pinch of saffron (optional)

For the dumplings
- 1 large egg, lightly beaten
- 100ml water
- 350g plain flour
- 250g pumpkin, peeled and diced very small
- ½ tsp coriander seeds, toasted and ground
- 1 tbsp dried barbaries
- 100g onion, finely diced
- 1/4 tsp pul biber
- fine sea salt, to taste
- black pepper, to taste
- 20g butter, diced into 2g pieces
- fresh herbs, to serve (I like a mixture of coriander, dill, tarragon and basil)

I grew up in the Greek part of Cyprus, and there was a restaurant in Limassol called The Syrian Club. I was taken there by Syrian friends, and I don't think I have ever (and to this day) eaten better mezze. Their shish kebabs were the juiciest and tabbouleh so vibrant and sharp, I am still trying to recreate it at home but it is never quite the same. I think they soaked their bulgur grains (which were very al dente) in lemon juice. In this dumpling dish I have attempted to marry dishes inspired by Central Asia, Azerbaijan and some Syrian flavours. Both Syrian and Azerbaijani cuisines have Turkic and Iranian influences. So here I add pul biber and barberries to recreate that wonderful zing and pleasant spiciness that I first encountered as a 13-year-old in The Syrian Club.

In a bowl, mix the eggs and water and gradually add in the flour. Mix well and knead on a well-floured surface until the dough stops sticking to your hands. You should end up with firm, elastic dough. Wrap it in cling film and rest in the fridge for 30 minutes.

Put all of the nage vegetables into a pot filled with 1.5 litres of cold water, season it well with salt, bring to the boil then lower the heat and simmer for about 20 minutes. You can now, if you have time, leave the vegetables in to infuse the stock further or strain the vegetables out immediately. Taste it for salt, it should be well seasoned. Grind some saffron (if using) with salt in a pestle and mortar and add this to the nage.

For the pumpkin, mix the diced pumpkin with the onions, coriander seeds and barberries, season really well with salt and a very generous grinding of black pepper and mix thoroughly with your hands.

Divide the dough into two parts and roll each one into a sausage shape. Then cut each sausage into ten 25g pieces.

Roll each piece into a rough 12cm circle. Place 1 tablespoon of the filling in the centre of each circle and a tiny piece of butter on top of the filling. Pull up the two opposite edges of the circle and stick them firmly together above the filling. Do the same with the two other edges, creating an X shape with the edges. Now join the "ears" by joining the corners, turning the X shape into an "8" shape.

Lightly grease a steamer with some flavourless oil and pop the dumplings in. Steam them for about 15 minutes or until the filling is cooked inside. Serve in the broth with the fresh herbs scattered over.

Photography by @Joe_Woodhouse

SPICED LENTIL SOUP V

Donated by Hemsley + Hemsley
@HemsleyHemsley

"We adore a lentil stew! From a spicy dahl to a split pea soup, a big pot of lentils is our kind of food. It's a simple, tasty, comforting meal for families, friends and those you love."

Serves 8

use organic ingredients where possible

For the soup

2 tbsp ghee or coconut oil
2 large red onions, diced
4 garlic cloves, finely diced
750g red lentils
1 tin tomatoes
1 tbsp fresh thyme leaves or 2 tsp dried thyme
1 tbsp fresh oregano or 2 tsp dried oregano
1 tbsp ground cumin
a pinch of aleppo chilli flakes (or to taste)
2 litres hot water
2 large pinches sea salt
black pepper, freshly ground
juice of 1 small lemon
1 tbsp pomegranate molasses

For the lemony herb oil

3 handfuls flat-leaf parsley
1 garlic clove
1 tsp fresh oregano leaves
5 tbsp extra-virgin olive oil
2 tbsp fresh lemon juice
sea salt
pepper

To serve

a pinch of aleppo chilli flakes (or to taste)
a small handful of pistachios (around 16)
a small handful of pomegranate seeds

We wanted to incorporate traditional Syrian spices into a hearty dish that still had a Hemsley stamp on it – so we chose warming aleppo chilli and balanced it out with cool pomegranate seeds and pistachios for added crunch. No H+H soup is complete without a vibrant green drizzle, so we added a swirl of our lemony herb oil.

In a large saucepan, gently fry the onions in ghee or coconut oil for 8 minutes until softened.

Add the garlic, thyme, oregano, cumin and chilli and continue to fry for a further 30 seconds, being careful not to let the spices burn.

Rinse the lentils and add to the pan with the tomatoes and hot water. Cover and bring to a simmer on a medium heat for 25 minutes, or until the lentils are tender.

Turn off the heat, add the sea salt, pomegranate molasses, lemon juice and black pepper to taste.

To make the lemony herb oil, finely chop all the ingredients with a knife or a food processor, and then stir through the extra-virgin olive oil and lemon juice at the last minute. Season to taste. The oil can be blended quite chunky or smooth, depending on your preference.

To serve, add a swirl of lemony herb oil, then top with crushed pistachios, pomegranate seeds and the chilli flakes.

Portrait by @NickHopper_GalaxyMan
Photography by @PatriciaNiven

SPINACH & LENTIL SOUP V

Donated by Jack Monroe
@MXJackMonroe

Serves 4-6

- 2 large onions
- 1 bulb garlic
- 1 tbsp cumin seeds
- ½ tsp mustard seeds
- ½ tsp chilli flakes, or less to taste
- 1 whole lemon
- 200g lentils
- 600ml stock
- 200g spinach
- a fistful of parsley or coriander

This soup is a variation on one I found many years ago in a cookbook called Saha, by Greg and Lucy Malouf. I lost the book to a good friend, but remember the basics of this simple, almost store-cupboard recipe, and over the years that followed I made it my own. It is a little fiddly, but completely worth it for its freshness and striking colour. I make it with green lentils, but it works equally well with split yellow peas, red lentils, cowpeas, black beans, chickpeas or any other pulse that you can think of.

First, rinse your lentils and pop into a saucepan that will easily take double their volume. Cover with cold water, do not add any salt at this stage as your lentils may seize and refuse to soften. Bring to the boil and reduce to a simmer, keeping an eye on them.

Peel and dice your onions and toss them into a new, large pot. Peel and roughly chop your garlic, add the cumin, mustard and chilli along with a slosh of oil or a knob of butter. Cook on a gentle heat to soften.

Finely chop your lemon, whole, rind and all, and toss it into the pot. Stir occasionally to prevent it from sticking and burning. Stuff the spinach and herbs into a blender with a little water, and pulse well to liquidise. It should be alarmingly green, bold and invigorating. Stand this to one side, you'll need it in a minute.

When your lentils are soft and swollen, drain and rinse them to knock off any residue that has formed on the surface. Tip them in with the onions and garlic. Cover in stock, bring to the boil and reduce to a simmer. Cook for a further 20 minutes or so to soften the lentils, the longer the better.

When ready to serve, pour in the bright green liquid. Stir well, and season to taste. You can eat the chunks of lemon, if you like, they're perfectly edible, and the sharp, bitter explosion is a welcome contrast to the deep earthiness of the cumin and lentils. This soup freezes well, and any leftovers will form an excellent base for a curry.

Beef and lamb

Poultry

5. MAINS FOR SHARING

"Whatever our background and whatever our differences, a meal shared can build a thousand bridges."

Amelia Freer

ALEPPO KOFTE KEBAB WITH BLACKENED CHILLI SAUCE

Donated by Josh Katz at Berber & Q

@BerberAndQ

"We have a real passion and love for Middle Eastern food, so to be able to use food as a vehicle to make a change is a fantastic opportunity."

Serves 4

1kg aged ribeye cap, cut into 3cm cubes (or minced by your butcher)

80g aleppo chilli flakes (pul biber)

15g garlic cloves

10g ground coriander

5g baharat spice mix

For the chilli sauce

5 large plum tomatoes, finely chopped

6 cloves garlic, crushed then finely chopped

3 grilled and blackened red chillies

20g aleppo chilli flakes

50ml olive oil

10ml red wine vinegar

seasoning to taste

Serve with warm pitta bread and garnish with dill

We've had a kofte pitta sandwich on our menu since we opened, and it has always been one of our favourites. We also know that Syrians are very fond of koftes, so it seemed like the perfect dish for us to adapt. The sauce they use with their kofte often has a sweetness to it, but a classic Syrian kofte sauce is made using sour cherries, adding a slight bitterness. We decided to sweeten ours with a drizzle of date syrup, which works well with the spiciness of the aleppo chilli.

Combine all the kebab ingredients and put them through a mincer.

Portion into 200g balls and skewer them on metal skewers.

Put them back in the fridge to set for an hour or two.

In the meantime, blacken the chillies on your barbecue or on a cast-iron griddle, then remove the stalks and finely chop.

Add the finely chopped tomatoes and minced garlic, then mix through the rest of the ingredients. Season to taste.

Grill the skewered kebabs on a barbecue or a griddle pan until slightly pink, then rest and remove the skewer.

Place the meat on toasted pitta bread, garnish with the sauce and some dill leaves.

Photography by @KatieWilsonFoto

MEATBALLS WITH BUTTERNUT SQUASH & TAHINI SAUCE

Donated by Itab Azzam and Dina Mousawi of Syria Recipes From Home
@ItabAzzam @DMousawi @Syria_RecipesFromHome

"We Syrians use a lot of fresh ingredients. We rely a lot on vegetables, so most meat dishes are actually like vegetable dishes with meat in it rather than the other way around. My husband is British and we talk about food a lot and I always say: 'Oh I'm going to make this today', and so I say the vegetable in the dish. And he'll say: 'Oh you mean the chicken dish?' and I'm like, 'No, it's not a chicken dish, it's a bean dish or an aubergine dish.' We appreciate vegetables a lot." – Itab

Serves 4

1 butternut squash, peeled
1/2 kg minced beef
1 onion
2 handfuls of parsley, finely chopped
2 tsp salt
1 tsp ground black pepper

For the sauce
1 small clove of garlic, crushed
2 tbs tahini
juice of 1 lemon
2 tbs yoghurt
2 tbs water
salt and pepper, to taste

For the topping
a handful of pine nuts
a knob of butter

In Syria, pumpkins grow in abundance, so every summer there's a new crop to find things to do with. Most people use them to make jam, but some of the tastiest pumpkin recipes are the savoury ones. In Aleppo the most famous one is pumpkin kebab while in Damascus it's abu basti, a pumpkin stew with chickpeas and tomato sauce. On the coast they dry it and keep it in jars to be used all year round; they also cut it into cubes and keep it on the windowsill, in the belief that it keeps the flies away.

Syrian pumpkin tastes sweeter and richer than it is British cousin, and that is why we are using butternut squash in this recipe as it is closer in taste. Pumpkin meatballs are a combination of some of the most quintessential Syrian ingredients put together on one plate

Pre heat the oven to 180C/350F/Gas mark 6. Cut the butternut squash into cubes, season with salt and pepper then roast until tender.

Using a food processor, finely chop the onions, followed by the parsley. Add both to the mince, salt and pepper then mix all together with your hands. Form into balls roughly the size of ping pong balls.

Roast the meatballs in the oven for 6-8 minutes or until browned.

Mix the tahini, yoghurt, lemon, water, garlic and salt all together in a bowl until it forms a very smooth consistency. If the mixture is too thick add a bit more water.

Heat a knob of butter in a frying pan and toast the pine nuts for a couple of minutes or until golden.

Layer the meat balls and the butternut squash in a serving bowl. Drizzle generously with the tahini sauce. You could leave a bit of the sauce to be served on the side.

Top with pine nuts.

Photography by @KatieWilsonFoto
Styling by @KloellaDeville
With thanks to Backgrounds Prop Hire

BEEF BRISKET KARI & SMOKED AUBERGINE RAITA

Donated by Hoppers
@HoppersLondon

"We took some inspiration from a traditional Syrian Christian beef curry and added a special Hoppers touch to it, bringing in some of our favourite Sri Lankan ingredients. It was fascinating to see how some Syrian dishes had many similarities to those we commonly find in Sri Lanka and the Indian subcontinent. Many ingredients, especially nuts like pistachios, almonds and walnuts, ethnic vegetables like okra and aubergines, and legumes like chickpeas and lentils are commonly used in our food as well, which made the process of developing our recipes very exciting."

Serves 4-6

For the beef

1kg beef brisket, cut into 1½ inch chunks
3 tsp fresh ginger, finely chopped
3 tsp garlic, finely chopped
4 medium banana shallots, sliced
4-5 green finger chillies, stalks removed
20 fresh curry leaves
4 tsp coriander powder
1 tsp turmeric powder
3 tsp red chilli powder
1½ tsp black pepper powder
3 + 2 tbsp coconut oil
salt, to taste

For the beef spice mix

8 green cardamom pods
1 x 3in cinnamon stick (Sri Lankan)
1 tsp fennel seeds
8 cloves
1 piece mace
1 star anise

For the smoked aubergine raita

1 cup greek yoghurt
1 medium japanese aubergine
½ tsp mustard seeds
½ tsp turmeric powder
1 green chilli, finely chopped
2 tsp vegetable oil
1 tbsp pomegranate seeds
salt, to taste

Marinate the meat in the fridge for 4-6 hours in one tablespoon of coconut oil, the turmeric and one teaspoon of salt.

Gently roast the ingredients for the spice mix in a pan over a slow heat, and once cooled, mix and grind them to a fine paste in a coffee grinder. Do not run the grinder for too long as it could get hot and burn the spices.

Heat 2 tablespoons of coconut oil in a large, thick-based casserole dish (ideally cast iron) over a medium heat and add the ginger, garlic and shallots. Fry them gently, stirring constantly until softened and brown.

Add the chilli and the coriander powder and fry them for a minute. Add a splash of water if they stick. Add the marinated beef and cook over a medium-high heat for 5 minutes, stirring every 30 seconds.

Add 3 cups of water, 1 teaspoon of salt and the green chillies and bring to a boil. Then immediately reduce to a gentle simmer, cover and cook over a low heat for around 90 minutes. Stir occasionally and add more water if needed.

If using a slow cooker, brown the meat first on the browning mode and then cook in the slow cooker for 8 hours, or until the meat is very tender.

When done, the meat should be very tender and the liquid should have reduced down to the consistency of a semi-thick curry. If you prefer a thinner consistency, feel free to add more water.

Heat 2 tablespoons of coconut oil over a medium heat and fry the curry leaves and ground spice mix for 30 seconds. Immediately stir this spiced oil into the curry.

Add the black pepper and check for seasoning, adding more salt if required. Cook for a final couple of minutes and serve hot.

Garnish with fried curry leaves or fried dried red chillies and eat with roti or steamed rice.

To make the Raita rub the aubergine all over with half teaspoon oil and place under the grill for 15 to 20 minutes, turning every few minutes. Remove when the aubergine is charred and soft. Leave to cool and then peel, slit in half, discard the hard seeds and mince the flesh.

Heat the remaining oil on medium heat and add mustard seeds. Once they splutter add turmeric and chilli and take off the heat immediately.

Mix all the ingredients well, season to taste and chill. Garnish with pomegranate seeds before serving.

Photography by @MarcusCobden

GRILLED AUBERGINE WITH BEEF KEEMA & PINE NUTS

Donated by Harneet Baweja and Nirmal Save at Gunpowder
@Gunpowder_London

"I wanted to create something everyone can enjoy, a celebration of humble flavours from humble origins – a well-balanced dish firmly rooted in Syrian cooking."

Serves 4

For the beef mince
4 tbsp vegetable oil
2-3 x 1in sticks of cinnamon
3-4 cardamom pods
4-5 cloves
2 medium onions, chopped
1 tbsp ginger, chopped
1 tbsp garlic, chopped
½ tsp turmeric powder
½ tsp red chilli powder
1 tsp cumin powder
2 tbsp coriander powder
3 medium tomatoes, chopped
½ tsp garam masala powder
800g beef, minced

For the grilled aubergines
2 big aubergines
1 tbsp vegetable oil
1 tbsp crushed black pepper

For the pine nut kachumber
200g pine nuts
1 bunch spring onions
1 tomato
2 green chillies, chopped
2 tsp coriander, chopped
yoghurt, optional
salt, to taste

Syrian cuisine is more similar to Indian cuisine than you might expect! I've taken inspiration from the dish mnazaleh be aswad, made of aubergine, minced lamb and pine nuts, and put my own spin on it. I've substituted baharat-spiced minced lamb for spiced Indian beef keema, balancing the dish out with kacumber, similar to the classic fattoush salad found throughout Syria.

Heat the vegetable oil in a thick-bottomed saucepan. Add the cinnamon, cardamom and cloves, sauté for half a minute, then add the chopped onions and sauté over a medium heat, stirring occasionally, until golden brown.

Add the chopped ginger and garlic, then stir well for a couple of minutes and add the turmeric, chilli, cumin and coriander powder and sauté for a further five minutes.

Add the chopped tomato and garam masala, then stir and allow to simmer for 10-15 minutes, or until the oil separates from the masala.

Add the mince and cook over a high heat for five minutes, stirring constantly. Lower the heat to a gentle simmer and leave covered for about 10 minutes.

Remove the lid, turn up the heat and sauté for a further 10 minutes, stirring constantly until almost dry.

Halve, season with pepper and then grill the aubergines for 4 minutes on each side.

Serve the beef mince on top of the grilled aubergine, then top with some yoghurt and a mix of all the chopped ingredients in the pine nut kachumber salad.

Photography by @KatieWilsonFoto

SYRIAN KOFTE, PICKLED WHITE CABBAGE, PRESERVED LEMON & YOGHURT PITTA SANDWICH

Donated by Josh Katz at Shawarma Bar
@ShawarmaBarLdn

"Allspice and cinnamon are classic spices to compliment lamb in Syria. We have spiced it up using aleppo chilli flakes, also a Syrian ingredient, commonly used in Turkey as well, where it is know as pul biber. We've added a bit more spice to the sauce using biber salcasi, a hot Turkish pepper paste."

Makes approximately 3 sandwiches

For the kofte
200g lamb mince
200g beef mince
60g breadcrumbs
1 tsp aleppo chilli flakes (also known as pul biber)
½ tsp cinnamon, ground
¼ tsp nutmeg, ground
¼ tsp white pepper, ground
¼ tsp allspice, ground
1 handful parsley, finely chopped
½ tsp black pepper, ground
½ tsp salt

For the kofte tomato sauce
20ml olive oil
½ an onion, finely diced
2 cloves garlic, minced
1 tsp aleppo chilli flakes
½ tsp cayenne pepper
1 tbsp biber salcasi (hot pepper paste)
800g tinned chopped tomatoes
3 tbsp date syrup
½ tsp white pepper, ground
½ tsp salt

For the pickled white cabbage
¼ white cabbage, thinly shredded
2 tsp table salt
125ml cider vinegar
100g caster sugar
1tsp cumin seeds
1tsp turmeric

For the tahini sauce
100g raw tahini
200ml ice-cold water
salt to taste

For the preserved lemon yoghurt
100g turkish yoghurt
25g preserved lemon flesh, very finely chopped
15ml olive oil
a pinch of maldon sea salt

For the herb salad
a small handful of picked dill leaves
a small handful of picked parsley leaves
a small handful of picked mint leaves
a small handful of thinly slice red cabbage

To serve
1 plum tomato, diced
1 long green chilli, diced
3 fresh pittas, round and fluffy if possible

Thinly slice the cabbage and sprinkle with the salt, leave for 1 hour. Dissolve the sugar in the vinegar on a gentle heat. Toast the cumin seeds in a dry frying pan. Once the sugar is dissolved in the vinegar, turn the heat off and add the toasted cumin seeds and turmeric to the liquor.

Once the cabbage has salted for 1 hour, rinse off the salt and pour over the liquor. You may need to weigh down the cabbage to make sure it is all submerged. Allow to cool and then store in an airtight container in your fridge.

To make the kofte sauce, sweat down the finely chopped onions, minced garlic and aleppo chilli flakes in the olive oil on a low heat for about 10 minutes. Then add the hot pepper paste, the white pepper, the salt and the cayenne pepper and cook for another 5 minutes. Stir in the chopped tomatoes and date syrup and cook on a low heat for 45 minutes-1 hour until thickened.

For the kofte, mix all the ingredients well in a bowl and roll into 6 rugby ball-shaped meatballs. Heat up a griddle pan, and when it is smoking hot, griddle the kofte balls, turning every few minutes to colour them on all sides. Place the meatballs in a small baking dish, cover with the sauce and bake in a preheated oven at 170C/325F/gas 3 for 30 minutes.

To make the sauce, put the tahini in a large mixing bowl. Gradually pour in the ice-cold water, mixing with a whisk until a smooth, sauce-like consistency, similar to double cream is achieved. Season to taste with salt.

Each sandwich should contain the koftes in tomato sauce, some tahini sauce, preserved lemon yoghurt, pickled white cabbage, herb salad, some diced tomatoes and a sprinkling of diced green chillies.

Photography by @TomsDinner

EST.2016

FATTEH'D MAKDOUS (STUFFED BABY AUBERGINES IN A TOMATO & YOGHURT SAUCE)

Donated by Dalia Dogmoch Soubra
@DaliasKitchen

Serves 6

12 baby aubergines
50g pine nuts
1 onion, finely chopped
1 onion, thinly sliced
300g minced lamb (preferably lean)
1 pinch of cinnamon
2 tomatoes
2 tbsp tomato paste
250ml water
1 pinch of sugar
1.5kg yoghurt
3 tbsp tahini
2 garlic cloves, minced
1 tbsp lemon juice
125ml water
½ tsp salt
½ tsp white pepper
200g arabic pitta bread
30g fresh parsley, chopped
30g toasted almonds (optional)
salt and pepper to taste
vegetable oil and butter for frying

Fatteh'd magdous is a classic Syrian dish. Fatteh comes from the Arabic way of saying to crumble or pull the bread over something, which is basically what this dish is. The different textures and bursts of flavour from the garlic tahini yoghurt, the soft aubergine and the crunch of the bread and nuts always remind me of our Syrian kitchen.

Cut the top off the aubergines and peel off a few strips of skin. This should reduce any bitterness.

Heat a frying pan over a low heat, add a little vegetable oil and fry the aubergines. They are ready when they are tender when poked with a fork. Depending on the size of the aubergines, this can take anywhere from 20 to 40 minutes.

In the meantime, fry the pine nuts in a little oil and butter until golden brown. Set aside.

In the same pan, add the finely chopped onions and cook until translucent before adding the minced lamb and cinnamon. Cook the meat for about 5 minutes, then add half the pine nuts and season. Set aside and keep warm.

In a saucepot, bring water to a simmer and gently drop in the tomatoes. Let them simmer for 60 seconds, remove them and, once cool enough to handle, peel, deseed and dice them.

Add a little oil to the empty saucepot and the thinly sliced onions and cook them for a few minutes before adding the tomato paste. Cook for another minute before adding the diced tomatoes, a pinch of sugar, and salt and pepper to taste. Add the cup of water, bring to a gentle boil, cover and simmer for 10-15 minutes.

In a bowl, whisk the yoghurt, tahini, garlic, lemon juice, water, salt and pepper. Set aside.

Cut or tear the pitta bread into small squares. Heat a frying pan with a little oil and butter, and toast the bread until golden brown.

Cut a long vertical opening in the middle of the aubergines and stuff them with the meat and pine nut mixture.

Using a deep and large serving plate, assemble the dish, starting with the toasted bread, then the yoghurt and the tomato sauce. Place the aubergines on top, sprinkle with the remaining pine nuts (and almonds if you desire) and the parsley.

Photography by @SukainaRajabali

1/3
CUP

KOOSA MAHSHI (STUFFED PEPPERS)

Donated by Sama Meibar
@Curly_Sama

"Everywhere you go in Syria, you are invited in to eat, every corner you turn, you are hit with the smell of something delicious cooking. Syrian cuisine is at the heart of the society, and food always brings people together."

Serves 6-7

1.5kg lebanese squash or bell peppers, washed and hollowed out

3-4 lemons

1 tin of chopped tomatoes

2 cloves of garlic, crushed

a handful of dried mint

For the filling

1 cup of glazed rice, washed

200g lamb, minced (including some fat)

½ tsp cumin

1 tsp seven spices

1 tsp salt

Stuffed peppers are one of my all-time favourite Syrian dishes and something that I still ask my mum to make every time I go back home. The dish is fairly simple so the key here is the Syrian seven spices – in Syria, every family goes to the spice market and gets their own unique blend of spices created for them. Spices in the Middle East are much stronger than spices in Europe so it's really worth getting the more expensive, better quality stuff to ensure that the flavour is strong.

Mix the ingredients for the filling together in a bowl.

Use the filling to stuff the squashes/peppers leaving about 2 cm empty at the top. (If using peppers, cut a circle around the stems but make sure to keep them as a lid for later.)

Layer the stuffed peppers in a large pot.

Pour in 1 litre of water and add the lemon juice (the mixture should taste sour).

Add the tin of chopped tomatoes.

Bring to the boil and then lower the heat to a simmer for 45 minutes.

Add the garlic and the mint, then bring back to the boil for a minute.

Take the peppers out of the liquid and serve. The liquid can be used as a kind of side soup.

Photography by @KatieWilsonFoto
Portrait by @CharlotteHuCo
Styling by @KloellaDeville

LAMB & SOUR CHERRY MEATBALLS

Donated by Ed Smith at Rocket and Squash
@RocketAndSquash

"I was inspired to create this dish by a postcard my brother added to my blog, Rocket and Squash, six years ago. It detailed some of the food that he had enjoyed whilst holidaying in Damascus and Aleppo. That included a photo of an Aleppo cherry kebab: marble-sized lamb meatballs in a glossy cherry sauce, which is apparently as sweet and sour as pomegranate molasses. It's fascinated me for years, and it's chilling and saddening to think how basic acts that would have been part of daily life just a few years ago, like heading to a local café, have been obliterated."

Serves 8

For the cherries

125g sour cherries, dried
300ml boiling water

For the meatballs

50g sour cherries, soaked and chopped
600g lamb mince
100g ricotta
1 large egg
50g panko breadcrumbs
15g fresh coriander, stems finely chopped, leaves reserved to garnish
1 heaped tsp cumin, ground
1 tsp mixed spice
1 tsp cinnamon, ground
black pepper
sunflower or vegetable oil, for frying

For the sour cherry sauce

300g medium onions, quartered
400g lamb stock
300g cherry juice, not from concentrate
the remaining soaked sour cherries and their water
1 tsp cornflour
2 tbsp sunflower or vegetable oil
sea salt
black pepper

To serve

coriander tops
plain rice
puffy flatbreads

I was definitely influenced by the Aleppo cherry kebab, though my meatballs are not even close to being authentic. Fresh sour cherries aren't abundant in the UK, so a combination of dried cherries and cherry juice provide the high notes. The meatballs themselves are bigger and probably lighter, as ricotta and breadcrumbs are part of the mix, not just lamb mince. I also serve them in a more savoury, onion and lamb sauce (although it's still sweet and sour) to go with rice and flatbread; in Aleppo, you'd just scoop them with flatbreads and eat, as the name suggests, with your fingers like a kebab.

Pour 300ml of boiling water over the dried sour cherries and leave to soak for 8 hours, or overnight. Remove 50g of now-plump cherries for the meatballs, and keep the remainder in the soaking liquid, as this forms part of the sauce.

Roughly chop the 50g pile of sour cherries. Drop them in a large mixing bowl, along with the lamb mince, ricotta, egg, breadcrumbs, coriander stems and spices. Mix thoroughly, then get your hands dirty and roll the meatballs to about the size of a walnut – 25g each if you're into measuring. Refrigerate until required, and for at least 30 minutes.

Meanwhile, make the sauce in a casserole dish or a high-sided sauté pan. Heat the oil over a medium-high heat. Place the onion quarters flat-side down and allow to brown before turning onto their second side, repeat the browning, then cook the curved side as well. The whole process will take 5-8 minutes in total, and the onion wedges will sweeten and soften as they cook.

Add the lamb stock, cherry juice, remaining sour cherries and their soaking liquid to the onions. Heat to a high simmer and allow to reduce and intensify for 15 minutes. During this time, remove 3 tablespoons of liquid from the pan and mix that in a mug with the cornflour. Pour this back into the pan and stir, it will help to thicken the sauce.

Fry the meatballs in a little oil, using a heavy-bottomed frying pan over a medium-high heat. You may need to do this in batches, depending on the size of your pan. Allow them to colour and get a little crust for 4-5 minutes, but not fully cook through. Then add, along with any cooking juices, to the cherry and lamb-stock sauce. Season with plenty of salt and black pepper and cook for 10 minutes more. Serve with plain rice, soft flatbread and coriander leaves.

With special thanks to Borough Market

Photography by @PatriciaNiven

LAMB TONGUE FATTEH

Donated by Tristram Bowden, pictured, & Lee Tiernan at Black Axe Mangal
@BlackAxeMangal @TristramBowden @LeeTiernan

Serves 4

For the bakken spice mix

This is a spice mix that we use a lot for lamb dishes at the restaurant. It's a blend of cumin, fennel, coriander, caraway, black pepper and a little star anise, toasted and ground.

For the lamb tongues

8 lamb tongues
50g rock salt
20g bakken spice mix, see above
4 cloves garlic, minced
a few sprigs of thyme
rendered lamb fat/olive oil

For the fatteh

500g greek yoghurt
100g strong tahini
200g chickpeas, soaked and cooked
20g bakken spice mix
2 lemons, juiced
salt, to taste

For the "sort of" green sauce

100g vine leaves, pickled
2 cloves garlic, minced
2 baby lemons, preserved
olive oil, to bind

To garnish

6 red chillies, charred, sliced and pickled
100g pine nuts, toasted
a pinch of paprika
50g butter, melted

Rub the tongues with salt, spice, garlic and thyme and leave for 2 hours. Then gently rinse them clean, submerge them in the warm fat and cover, cooking for approximately 1 hour at 120C/250F. They should fall off a skewer under their own weight. Peel while warm and set aside to cool in the fat.

We use our own smoked-potato sourdough for the flatbread, but suggest that you use 4 pitta breads, toasted and ripped into pieces.

For the fatteh, mix the yoghurt with the tahini, spice mix, chickpeas and the lemon juice. If the mixture is a little thick, you can add some of the water left over from cooking the chickpeas.

For the "sort of" green sauce, chop the vine leaves very fine to break them down, then do the same with the whole preserved, deseeded lemons. Mix together with the garlic and bind with a good splash of olive oil, this should resemble a green sauce.

To assemble, place the toasted bread in a large dish and sprinkle with a little of the chickpea cooking water to soak, then pour over the yoghurt and tahini mixture. (This should lie flat.)

Slice the tongues in half and cook on a very hot griddle pan to get colour and texture, then scatter over the yoghurt mixture.

To finish, pour the melted butter over evenly and scatter the pickled chilli and toasted pine nuts. Then add a light dusting of paprika and serve with a little of the vine leaf and lemon green sauce for a lift.

Photography by @PatriciaNiven

MUKLOUBI BI LAHMI (UPSIDE-DOWN LAMB CAKE)

Donated by Saima Khan
@HampsteadKitchn

"I love how one dish could take a week's worth of preparation, from sourcing the right ingredients, marinating, slow cooking and smoking the meats. Quite often there are handful of spices used, but a recipe can change drastically depending on at what point they are added to the dish, whether they are roasted or boiled with water to intensify the flavours."

Serves around 8

1kg lamb loin cut into 2cm cubes with the fat trimmed

700g aubergines cut into ¼inch-thick slices

50g seven spice mixture (see below)

1 cinnamon stick

2 bay leaves

juice of ½ a lemon

a few glugs of vegetable oil

50g clarified butter

500g long-grain rice (wash the rice at least 5 times until the water is clear, then soak for a minimum of 30 minutes)

90g pine nuts

For the seven spice mixture

1 tsp sweet paprika

2 tsp group cumin

1 tsp ground coriander

1 tsp ground nutmeg

1 tsp cinnamon

1 ground allspice berry

2 tsp ground black pepper

I first had this dish in Syria, I was homesick and desperate to meet a family and enjoy a good meal. I recall eating this dish with a beautiful lady called Soraya, and I ate until I couldn't move. I adapt this dish sometimes by scattering over pomegranates and rose petals and serving it with muhammara and na na wa jorz dips.

Cut the aubergines into slices, cover with cold water and salt. Soak for half an hour, then place on sheets of clean kitchen paper and leave to dry for a few hours. I usually do this overnight.

In a pan, combine the lamb with the spice mix, lemon juice, cinnamon stick, bay leaves and salt.

Bring to the boil, then cover and cook on a slow heat for about 2 hours until the lamb is soft and tender. I use a pressure cooker to speed this process along in only 45 minutes.

In another pan, heat the vegetable oil, make sure it is sizzling hot and then fry the aubergine, leaving the cooked slices on kitchen roll to soak up any excess oil.

Heat the butter in a deep pan, making sure that it doesn't brown, then stir in the rice and make sure that it is coated in butter.

In a casserole dish, add a layer of the lamb (but leave the lamb stock to one side) then build up alternating layers of rice, aubergine and then more lamb.

Pour over the lamb stock so that the rice is covered.

Cover with a tightly sealed lid, and cook over a low heat for 30 minutes, until you see the rice swell up and the liquid reduce.

In another pan, fry the pine nuts with the remaining butter and dry them out on sheets of kitchen paper.

Put a flat serving dish under the casserole dish and flip the dish upside down.

Scatter the pine nuts over the top and serve with natural yoghurt.

Photography by @KatieWilsonFoto
Styling by @KloellaDeville

SHAKRIYEH (LAMB SHANKS & HOT YOGHURT STEW)

Donated by Dalia Dogmoch Soubra
@DaliasKitchen

Serves 6

- 6 lamb shanks, trimmed of excess fat
- 3 litres of hot water
- 2 onions, peeled and quartered
- 3 bay leaves
- 2 cinnamon sticks
- a handful of cardamom seeds (around 6g)
- a generous pinch of cloves (around 3g)
- 2 tsp salt
- 2 tsp white pepper
- 2kg yoghurt
- 1 egg
- 2 tbsp cornflour
- 175g vermicelli
- 375g short-grain rice, rinsed
- 50g pine nuts
- cracked black pepper
- 5 spring onions
- 12 radishes

Whenever there was a festive occasion, the Syrian women in my family would make this incredible dish. The lamb is simmered until it is tender in aromatics, which infuses the meat with wonderful flavour. Syrian dishes are often made with yoghurt sauces. In this case the yoghurt is hot, and the most important part of the recipe is that it does not split in the cooking process. My mother insists that the yoghurt needs to be newly opened from its container, that you have to stir the yoghurt in one direction only and that you may not taste the yoghurt before it boils fully. I still follow these directions while making shakriyeh – and the yoghurt indeed never splits.

Place the lamb shanks in a large pot filled with boiling water. Add the onions, bay leaves, cinnamon sticks, cardamom, cloves, half the salt and half the pepper to the water.

Bring to a boil, reduce the heat to low, cover and simmer for about 2-2 ½ hours or until the lamb is tender. Skim the fat that surfaces to the top of the water using a spoon to leave a clear broth for the end. In the meantime, make the rice by adding a little butter and vegetable oil to a pot. Add the vermicelli and fry until golden brown.

Add the rice, stir to combine then fill with water and cook the rice as directed on the pack, usually about 20 minutes, covered on a low heat. Keep the rice warm once it is cooked.

In the meantime, heat another frying pan over a medium heat, add a little oil and butter, and then fry the pine nuts until golden brown. Place them on a plate lined with paper napkins.

Once the lamb is ready, remove the shanks from the pot and keep them warm. You can take the meat off the bones or serve them whole.

Pour the cooking liquid through a sieve and discard the onions and aromatics. Set the strained broth aside.

In a large pot, whisk the yoghurt with the egg, cornflour, remaining salt and pepper and 250ml of the strained cooking liquid (add more if you desire).

Turn on the heat and, stirring constantly, cook the yoghurt over a low heat until it comes to a simmer. Cook it for another 2 minutes once it boils, then turn off the heat.

Place the lamb shanks in a large and deep serving dish, cover with the hot yoghurt, pine nuts and finish with cracked black pepper on top. Serve the shakriyeh with rice, fresh spring onions and radishes on the side.

Photography by @SukainaRajabali

GRILLED MARINATED NECK OF LAMB WITH PISTO & HUMMUS

Donated by José Pizarro
@Jose_Pizarro

"For me it's so important to be involved in #CookForSyria. There is nothing better than bringing people together around food. Food brings happiness and Syria, in this moment, needs a lot of happiness."

Serves 4

4 lamb-neck fillets

For the marinade
1 clove garlic, finely chopped
½ tbsp pimentón de la vera
1 tbsp honey
1 tsp cinnamon
1 tsp cumin
5 tbsp olive oil
a pinch of fresh oregano
black pepper, to taste

For the hummus
200g dried chickpeas
1 tsp bicarbonate of soda
5 tbsp tahini
juice of ½ a lemon
2 cloves garlic, crushed
a pinch of ground cumin
a pinch of za'atar
salt, to taste

For the vegetable pisto
4 tbsp olive oil
1 large onion, halved and chopped
1 red pepper, seeded and diced
2 garlic cloves, finely chopped
1 tsp ground cumin
½ tsp crushed dried chillies
1 x 300g aubergine, cut into 2cm pieces
200g courgettes, cut into small cubes
400g skinned and chopped tomatoes, fresh or from a can
a pinch of hot pimentón
black pepper, freshly ground
sea salt flakes

Middle Eastern spices with Spanish pimento and paprika work so well together. When you try this dish at home you will fall in love. It is a simple dish but full of lovely flavors. A fillet of neck of lamb marinated in spices from the Middle East with pisto and finished off with hummus. The recipe is very simple, it introduces spices like cumin and chilli in both the pisto and the lamb marinade and finishes off with a silky hummus to taste.

Soak the chickpeas with plenty of water and the bicarbonate of soda for 24 hours.

Meanwhile, put all the ingredients for the marinade together in a bowl, add the lamb necks and leave to marinate in the fridge for at least 5 hours.

Drain the chickpeas and place in a large pan, cover with fresh water, bring to the boil and simmer for up to 3 hours until they are tender and easy to mush. Add more boiling water if the level starts to get low. Leave the chickpeas to cool in the water and then drain, reserving some of the cooking liquid. Mix the tahini with half the lemon juice and add enough cooled cooking liquid to make a paste. Puree the paste and the chickpeas. Add the cumin, salt and lemon juice to taste, and more of the cooking liquid to give a soft texture.

Meanwhile, heat the oil in a large frying pan over a medium heat. Add the onion and red pepper, cover and cook gently for 7-8 minutes until soft and lightly golden. Uncover, stir in the garlic, cumin and dried chilli and cook for 1 minute. Stir in the aubergine, re-cover and cook for 6-8 minutes until beginning to soften, then stir in the courgettes, season with salt and cook for another 4 minutes. Stir in the tomatoes, 150ml water and some salt and pepper and simmer uncovered for 7-8 minutes until all the vegetables are tender and the sauce has reduced and thickened slightly. Keep warm until ready to serve.

Heat the oven to 190C/375F/gas 5. Heat a large frying pan to medium heat, place the lamb necks in and seal. You don't need oil in the pan as this will come from the marinade. Caramelise the necks then place in the oven for 2-4 minutes until medium rare, leave to rest for 2 minutes. Slice the lamb and put on top of the pisto with a dollop of hummus, a drizzle of extra-virgin olive oil and a sprinkling of za'atar.

Photography by @CharlotteHuCo

FREEKEH WITH LAMB FILLET

Donated by Imad Alarnab
@imadssyriankitchen

200g freekeh
400g water
800g lamb fillet
100g peas
2 tablespoons vegetable oil
2 tablespoons butter
Pepper
Salt
a bunch of fresh thyme

In Syrian culture, food is at the centre of everything. We can't make any journey without first planning the food. If you make a plan to go to the cinema, you plan what you'll eat. If you make a plan to visit your mother, you know what you're going to eat. There's no going out without eating something. Freekeh with lamb fillet is a dish most commonly served at weddings and celebrations. For Syrians, lamb fillet is the number one kind of meat. Freekeh is a cereal made from green durum wheat that is roasted and rubbed to create its unique smoky flavor.

Season the lamb fillet with salt and pepper.

Put two table spoons of vegetable oil and one table spoon of butter in a cooking pot.

Fry the lamb fillet till browned in the cooking pot.

Remove the lamb from the cooking pot and leave it on the side to rest.

Now put the peas and the freekeh in the same cooking pot and stir fry them for 5 minutes.

Add water, salt, and pepper. When the water starts boiling, covet the pot and lower the cooker's temperature. Leave it for 15 minutes.

Add one table spoon of butter and cover the pot again for ten more minutes.

Bake the lamb fillet in the oven for 8 minutes on 200°. When done, take the lamb out and let it rest for 10 minutes.

Serve the freekeh on a plate with lamb fillet and fresh thyme of top of it.

Optional: add shadow fried cashew nuts and pine nuts.

Photography by @hassanakkad

MUTTON "AL PASTOR", MUHAMMARA, TAHINI & MEDJOOL DATES

Donated by Nud Dudhia, pictured, and Chris Whitney at Breddos Tacos
@BreddosTacos

"The best bit about Syrian cuisine is the wonderful use of spice!"

Serves 4

For the mutton

1 mutton shoulder

1 tbsp cumin seeds, toasted and crushed in a pestle and mortar or spice mill

1 tbsp dried mexican oregano

10 pasilla oaxaqueno chillies, toasted in a dry frying pan until fragrant, then soaked in water for 30 minutes and drained

10 guajillo chillies, toasted in a dry frying pan until fragrant, then soaked in water for 30 minutes and drained

15 arbol chillies, toasted in a dry frying pan, then soaked in water for 30 minutes and drained

2 small onions, peeled and coarsely chopped

15 garlic cloves, peeled

100ml grapefruit juice

100ml orange juice

3 tbsp sea salt

For the muhammara

2 red peppers, roasted and peeled

2 jalapeño chillies, seeded and diced

2 tsp lemon juice, freshly squeezed

2 tsp ground cumin

2 tsp sea salt

4 tbsp pomegranate molasses

1 tbsp aleppo red pepper flakes

8 tbsp olive oil

2 cups walnuts, lightly toasted in a dry frying pan

For the dates

300g medjool dates, pitted and chopped into small pieces

100g butter

To serve

100g toasted walnuts, crushed

tahini, to taste

aleppo red pepper flakes

your favourite hot sauce

corn tortillas

coriander leaves

Al pastor is a dish adapted by Mexicans following a large Lebanese immigration to Mexico in the 1930s. In essence the Mexicans took the idea of a shawarma and applied their own pork, spices and herbs to the dish, cooking it on a vertical spit just like the Lebanese. For my dish I applied Mexican Al Pastor spices to mutton, cooked it on the same vertical spit and served it with some Syrian condiments. We used muhammara as a 'salsa' for our taco and included jalapeño in the mix to bring a little bit of Mexican to the table!

Put all the ingredients for the mutton apart from the meat itself in a blender and whizz on high until evenly mixed. Rub the mix all over the shoulder and marinate in the fridge for at least 24 hours. Remove it from the fridge at least 2 hours before you're ready to cook.

If you're using an oven, preheat it to 130C/250F/gas ½, place the mutton in a baking tray and cover with tinfoil. Bake for 5-6 hours and check for tenderness. It might need another 30 minutes to an hour depending on your oven. If you're using a smoker, set it for 15C/59F, then smoke the mutton for around 9 hours.

In the meantime, add all ingredients for the muhammara except for the olive oil in a blender and pulse, slowly adding the oil until combined. Try to maintain a chunky texture. Then fry the medjool dates with the butter until fragrant and slightly roasted.

When the mutton is tender, take it out of the oven or smoker and rest for at least 30 minutes. Then pull off the bone and chop into small 2-3cm pieces. Add any leftover marinade.

Warm up the tortillas in some butter, then top with some mutton, followed by a spoonful of muhammara, a drizzle of tahini, a sprinkle of the red pepper flakes, a couple of medjool dates, crushed walnuts, hot sauce and the coriander leaves. A squeeze of lime wouldn't go amiss either.

Photography by @CharlotteHuCo

AMAZING SPICED CHICKEN KEBABS WITH TAHINI YOGHURT, SUMAC FLATBREADS & POMEGRANATE

Donated by Jamie Oliver
@JamieOliver

"Food has the power to unite people, families and communities"

Serves 6

For the spiced chicken kebabs

3 cardamom pods
½ tsp cumin seeds
½ tsp coriander seeds
½ tsp ground cinnamon
½ tsp ground allspice
½ tsp sumac
½ tsp sweet smoked paprika
½ tsp dried thyme
2 cloves garlic
2 heaped tbsp thick natural yoghurt
olive oil
8 free-range chicken thighs, skin on, bone out
2 onions
2 lemons
6 fresh bay leaves

For the flatbreads

400g plain flour, plus extra for dusting
½ tsp baking powder
extra-virgin olive oil
sumac

For the tahini sauce

1 clove garlic
2 tbsp tahini
200ml thick natural yoghurt
1 lemon
1 pomegranate

This is food to share with friends. The quantities here are for six people, but you can easily scale up for a crowd, just keep the ratio of lemon, bay, onion and chicken the same. If you can, get outside and cook these on the barbecue for the most incredible smoky flavour that goes beautifully with the cooling tahini yoghurt and sweet pops of pomegranate. It's a real joy to eat.

Crush the cardamom pods. Put the seeds in a dry frying pan on a medium heat with the other spices and the thyme. Toast for 2 minutes, then crush in a pestle and mortar, seasoning generously with sea salt and black pepper. Peel and pound in the garlic, then stir through the yoghurt and a drizzle of olive oil. Halve the chicken thighs, then massage the marinade all over. Cover and refrigerate for 2 hours, or ideally overnight.

For the flatbreads, mix the flour, baking powder, a little salt, 1 tbsp of extra-virgin olive oil and 200ml of cold water in a large bowl, adding extra water if necessary. Knead on a floured surface until smooth, then return to the bowl, cover with a clean damp tea towel and put aside.

For the sauce, crush the garlic into a serving bowl. Add the tahini and yoghurt, finely grate in the lemon zest, squeeze in half the juice, then mix and season to perfection. Halve the pomegranate, then – holding one half cut-side down – bash the back of it with a spoon so that the seeds tumble over the sauce. Drizzle with extra-virgin olive oil.

Peel and quarter the onions, then separate into petals. Cut the lemon into 6 wedges. Get 3 skewers, thread a lemon wedge and a bay leaf onto each, then skewer on the chicken, interspersing with petals of onion. Finish each with a lemon quarter and bay leaf, then drizzle with olive oil. Place on a screaming hot griddle pan, then reduce to a medium heat and cook for 15 to 20 minutes, or until golden, gnarly and cooked through, turning regularly. Slice the meat off the skewers, to serve.

Meanwhile, divide the dough into 6 equal balls and roll out as thinly as you can. Mix 75ml of olive oil with 2 tsp of sumac and brush over each flatbread. Griddle for 1 to 2 minutes on each side, brushing with more sumac oil and sprinkling with salt when you turn.

Serve the kebabs and flatbreads with the tahini sauce, a selection of pickled veg and chillies and some shredded crunchy salad. You could even go all out and crush up some toasted nuts and drizzle over some pomegranate molasses for a deliciously sticky crunch. Enjoy!

Photography by @JamesLyndsay
Portrait by @DavidLoftus

BAKED CHICKEN & ALMOND MEATBALLS

Donated by Amelia Freer
@AmeliaFreer

"I was fortunate to go to Syria when I was 16 years old and spend a summer there. I fell in love with it – the architecture, vibe and of course the food! As a young girl who had only really camped in France, it was a wildly exciting experience. It feels like a truly joyful cuisine, and one that I am excited to include into my repertoire of cooking."

Serves 4

For the almond sauce

150ml chicken stock
1 lemon, zested
100g almond butter
salt to taste

For the meatballs

500g skinless, boneless chicken thighs, roughly chopped and then pulsed in a food processor (alternatively, you could use skinless chicken breasts)
1 egg, beaten
4 spring onions, finely sliced
6 tbsp almonds, ground
2 tbsp fresh coriander leaves, finely chopped
1½ tsp cumin, ground
1 tsp coriander, ground
black pepper, freshly ground
salt, freshly ground
olive oil, for brushing

This beautifully flavoured dish is ideal for sharing with loved ones. Any leftovers are perfect for lunch the next day too, so it might be a good idea to make a few more than you think you'll need. They work brilliantly piled on top of brown rice or tricolour quinoa, alongside a generous pile of greens, dressed simply with olive oil and lemon juice. Alternatively, you could make up a double batch, and serve them as a canapé with the almond sauce in a little dish for dipping.

To make the almond sauce, bring the chicken stock to the boil, then remove from the heat. Very slowly add small amounts of this to a bowl of almond butter and whisk well to combine. Continue adding the stock to the almond butter until you have the consistency of double cream. Stir through the lemon zest, season with salt and set to one side.

For the meatballs, first preheat the oven to 200C/400F/gas 6. Combine all the meatball ingredients together in a large bowl, mix and season well with salt and pepper.

Using damp hands, roll the mixture into tablespoon-sized balls (you should make around 16) and place on a large, greased baking tray. Brush the tops with olive oil and then bake for 17-20 minutes, or until cooked all the way through.

To serve, gently warm the almond sauce again. Plate up your meatballs, and serve drizzled with the almond sauce. Perhaps tear off a few more coriander leaves to garnish. Enjoy!

Photography by @KatieWilsonFoto

FATTI DAJAJ (POACHED CHICKEN WITH SPICED RICE, CRISPY BREAD & YOGHURT SAUCE)

Donated by Gizzi Erskine
@GizziErskine

Serves 6 (as a normal supper) or 8 (as part of a party dish)

For the chicken

1 free-range or organic chicken
1 stalk cinnamon
5 cloves
1 tsp black peppercorns
3 bay leaves
1 garlic bulb, cut in half
1 onion, quartered

For the sauce

1 onion, finely chopped
5 garlic cloves, peeled and finely chopped
2 tbsp butter or ghee
2 tsp cumin
2 tsp ground coriander
½ tsp hot paprika
3 green cardamom pods, lightly crushed
500ml greek yoghurt

For the rice

250g basmati rice
1 tbsp butter or ghee
reserved spiced chicken stock

To serve

1-2 pitta breads
reserved spiced chicken stock
butter or vegetable oil, for frying
a handful of flaked almonds
a handful of pine nuts
seeds of 1 pomegranate
a large handful of flat-leaf parsley leaves
a large handful of mint leaves

I grew up with Syrian friends; the Hakims. My elder sister was the same age as the eldest daughter, Sara, and my younger sister and I were a similar age to the younger daughter, Hannah. Their father, Karim, would cook Syrian food. I used to love going round there, even if only for this buttery rice he would make that would crisp up on the bottom. Ironically, his children preferred English food. Fatti dajaj comes in many guises. I've used a classic Syrian technique and then added some fun modern slants to make it more me.

Put the chicken, spices, bay leaves, garlic and onion into a large pot and fill with water until just covering the chicken. Place a lid on the pot and bring to the boil for 15 minutes, then simmer for 45.

Remove the chicken, onion and garlic and reduce the sauce by half over a high heat. Set aside. Once the chicken has cooled enough to handle, remove the skin and set aside, followed by all of the meat.

For the chicken skin, preheat the oven to 200C/400F/gas 6. Lay the skin on a baking tray, place another one on top, and bake for 20 minutes. You can toast your almonds and pine nuts on the top tray for the last 5 minutes. When done, sprinkle with a little salt and then cut into bite-sized shards.

Next, fry the rice in a tablespoon of butter for 3 minutes, and then cover over with your reserved stock. Put a lid on the pan and bring to a boil for 8 minutes, then take off the heat and allow to continue steaming under the lid for another 15 minutes.

To make the sauce, melt the butter or ghee in a pan over a medium heat, then add the onions and garlic and sweat for 15 minutes. Add the spices and fry for a further minute or two. Pour in a litre of the reduced stock and simmer for a further 25 minutes, until almost syrupy. Take it off the heat and let it cool for 10 minutes. Stir in the yoghurt and season.

Finally, slice the pitta bread into strips. Soak in a good few tablespoons of stock, then shallow fry in as much butter or ghee as you need until crisp and golden.

Layer your rice on a large platter, followed by the chicken. Next, pour over the sauce, followed by the pomegranate seeds. Roughly chop the almonds and season with salt, before sprinkling on to the dish with the pine nuts, then roughly chop together the mint and parsley leaves and scatter all over, followed by the crispy chicken skin.

Arrange the pitta bread pieces around the edge and serve!

Photography by @KatieWilsonFoto
Styling by @KloellaDeville

GRILLED QUAIL WITH GREEN HARISSA, POMEGRANATES & DATES

Donated by Nieves Barragán Mohacho at Barrafina
@BarrafinaLondon

"I went to the Middle East a couple of months ago and I fell in love with the food and the people."

Serves 4

4 quails, cut in half and deboned
8 garlic cloves, crushed with the skins left on
2 bay leaves
2 dried chillies
80g green harissa
100ml pomace olive oil (for the marinade)
1 shallot, finely chopped
40ml arbequina olive oil
20ml muscatel vinegar
4 large medjool dates, peeled and pitted
300ml chicken stock
2 tbsp coriander, chopped
salt and pepper to taste

In Spain we use something in cooking called mojo verde, which is a mixture of cumin, garlic, and coriander. I mixed some of the mojo verde with green harissa and it was incredibly tasty. Like Syrians, Spaniards also love dates and pomegranates, so we used them to make a nice salad with the quail.

Mix together the pomace olive oil, bay leaves, dried chillies and garlic.

Place the quail halves in the mixture and leave for two hours to marinate.

In a separate bowl, mix together the pomegranate seeds, shallots, coriander, arbequina olive oil and muscatel vinegar to form a dressing. Set aside.

In a medium-hot pan, add the chicken stock and the dates. Keep stirring the sauce until the dates have dissolved and the sauce becomes thick (about 4-5 minutes).

In a medium-hot pan, cook the quail, skin on, for 3-4 minutes, then turn around and cook for another two minutes. The quail should be cooked medium.

On a large plate, put the green harissa and then the quail (skin-side up). Pour over the date sauce, then the pomegranate and coriander dressing.

Photography by @Joe_Woodhouse

GUINEAFOWL WITH LENTILS, ZA'ATAR & LABNEH

Donated by Ollie Templeton at Carousel
@TempletonOllie @Carousel_Ldn

"The dish was inspired by my time working at Moro, when I started there, I would be on the early shift, usually working through the night, or starting extremely early, getting the breads cooked in the wood oven, and making the mezze."

Serves 4-6

1 tbsp toasted sesame seeds
1 tbsp wild thyme
1 tbsp wild mint
1 tbsp wild marjoram
1 tbsp sumac
1 tsp salt labneh
4 litres full-fat milk
1 litre heavy cream
500g cultured yoghurt
salt, to taste
1 muslin cloth

For the lentils
1kg lentils
1 onion
2 cloves garlic
2 tbsp cumin seeds
1 bunch coriander
200ml extra-virgin olive oil

For the guineafowl
1 guineafowl
2 tbsp labneh
1 tbsp za'atar

Syrian lentils were a staple at Moro. Lentils cooked with lots of toasted cumin, coriander and finished in a sizzling pan of golden garlic. So I thought that it would be nice to make it again as it's been years. The guineafowl stuffed with labneh works so well with the lentils, then as the meat rests, the juices mix with the labneh and create a lovely sour sauce.

Reduce 4 litres of milk by a third, add 1 litre of heavy cream and allow to cool until 27C/80F, then stir in cultured yoghurt and leave somewhere warm overnight.

In the morning, take the yoghurt and season liberally with salt, then hang in a muslin cloth overnight again. Now you have your labneh.

The lentils need to have been soaked overnight. Then in the morning, cook them in water with onions, garlic and bay leaves. Once al dente, drain them.

Chop 2 cloves of garlic and fry them in the olive oil. Once softened on a low temperature, add the cumin seeds whole and turn up the heat. Chop the coriander and add to the garlic and it will bubble up, then add the cooked lentils and stir. Check for seasoning.

Take the guineafowl off the carcass, keeping the leg and breast meat attached with the skin. Bone out the leg and thigh meat. Roast the bones and, when golden, make a stock with one onion and some more garlic and cumin seeds.

Lift the meat from the skin and stuff the labneh between, then press the meat back against it, do this with both the breast and the leg/thigh meat.

On a low heat, start browning the skin until crispy and caramelised. Once the skin is crispy, turn the meat over then add the lentils and stock and cook in the oven at 180C/350F/gas 4 for 6 minutes until the meat is cooked but juicy. Rest somewhere warm for another 5 minutes.

To serve, simply pour the lentils on to a plate, then place the guineafowl on top with an extra spoonful of the labneh and a sprinkle of za'atar.

Photography by @HannahIndia.Photography
Portrait by @OlegTolstoy

PHEASANT THIGH, POMEGRANATE & ALEPPO CHILLI

Donated by James Lowe at Lyle's
@LoweJames @LylesLondon

Makes enough for 6 skewers

3 hen pheasants
1 litre of water
80g salt
30g sugar
4 pomegranates
200g yoghurt
100g sumac
200g butter
aleppo chilli flakes

I started reading about Syrian cuisine and discovered lots of things that I was familiar with, but lots that were completely new to me. There is a simplicity to the food, a love of key spices and fruits, bold flavours and lots of grilling and roasting. I decided to go with pheasant and I rarely get the chance to play around with spicing with these kinds of ingredients. I tried to stay true to the spicing and sweet/sour elements of their food, with the chillis, sumac and pomegranate.

First, hang the yoghurt in some muslin over a strainer for 5 hours. Once firm, mix through with chopped sumac and season.

Make a brine by warming the water to 40C/105F and whisking in the salt and sugar until dissolved. Chill this in the fridge. Soak the thighs in the brine for 2 hours and then remove to a dry cloth.

For the pomegranates, remove the seeds and juice the fruit in a juicer. Reduce the juice to a third of its original amount.

Next, put the butter in a heavy-based pan and boil until it starts to turn brown and smell nutty. Pour through a strainer and reserve only the clear fat.

To prepare the pheasant, remove the legs from the birds. Cut the leg at the knee to separate the drumstick from the thigh. Take the thigh bone out by carefully cutting down either side of it. You want to leave the thigh in one piece, so make sure that you don't cut through the meat too much.

Place one thigh skin-side down on a chopping board. Turn it so that the thigh bone runs parallel to the edge of the table. Get two long skewers and thread them through either side of the thigh, first by piercing through the skin, and then the meat. Repeat with the rest of the thighs.

Brush the thigh with the brown butter and reduced pomegranate juice. Place above the coals on a barbecue so that it is not in direct contact with the grill. After the skin has crisped up and browned, flip over and finish the cooking.

Warm the remainder of the pomegranate juice and add brown butter. Use this as your sauce, it should be very sweet and sour.

Season the yoghurt with chillis and serve. We will be experimenting with several garnishes, beginning with fermented red cabbage and grilled sourdough bread.

Photography by @PatriciaNiven
Portait by @KatieWilsonFoto

POMEGRANATE-GLAZED GUINEAFOWL, WITH DATE & TAMARIND SAUCE

Donated by Greg Marchand at Frenchie Covent Garden
@FrenchieCoventGarden

"We are inspired by the 'richesse' of the Middle Eastern culture, the Mediterranean products and the "mezze" way to eat and cook. We love cooking for others. Cooking is sharing. Today, Syrians need our help, comfort and love. All these ingredients are in our cuisine. "

Serves 4

For the brine

295g water
75ml white wine vinegar
125g granulated sugar
6 tbsp fine sea salt
1 tsp mustard seeds
2 garlic cloves, crushed
1 bunch thyme

For the meat

1 small guineafowl, butchered, or 2 skin-on boneless free-range chicken breasts and 2 skin-on boneless free-range chicken thighs
1 tbsp grapeseed oil
1 tbsp unsalted butter
1 bottle pomegranate molasses

For the sauce

500g medjool dates
200g tamarind
3 limes

For the carrots and barley

1 kg carrots, for juicing
1 kg sandy carrots, for pureeing
1 orange, freshly juiced
1 pomegranate
harissa, to taste
barley, to serve 4
dried capers
almonds
grapes (dried or fresh)
shallots, fried
lemon zest

We really wanted to cook pomegranate, tamarind and date to go with guineafowl. We like the Syrian way to propose a dish with sweet and savoury ingredients. In Europe, we are not used to eating meat with pomegranate... and we love this contrast. Your palate will be surprised by the freshness of the pomegranate and the citrus, the brightness of the tamarind, and will feel soothed by the sweetness of the date puree.

If possible, have a butcher cut up a whole small guineafowl for you. Alternatively, you can use skin-on, boneless chicken breasts and thighs.

If you are using chicken, it's essential to get organic free-range chicken and to cook it with its skin on until it is crisp. The chicken breast needs to have the wing bone left intact, a cut sometimes called a supreme. A butcher should be able to prepare this for you.

For the brine, combine the water, vinegar, sugar, salt, mustard seeds, garlic and thyme in a medium, non-reactive saucepan and bring to a boil, stirring to dissolve the sugar and salt. Let cool, then refrigerate until cold.

Put the guineafowl into a large, deep bowl. Add the brine, making sure that the meat is submerged, and refrigerate until cold. Drain the guineafowl, then rinse under cold water and pat dry with paper towels. Refrigerate.

Around 30 minutes before you are ready to cook the guineafowl, take it out of the refrigerator and pat dry. Then heat a very large skillet over a medium-high heat, add the grapeseed oil and heat in the pan.

Add the guineafowl pieces, skin-side down, then reduce the heat to medium and cook for 12 minutes, or until the meat is almost cooked through (lower the heat slightly if necessary).

Glaze the skin of the guineafowl with pomegranate molasses.

For the date and tamarind sauce, blend the dates with the fresh tamarind, lime juice and lime zest. Add a little bit of water to the mixture to loosen it up.

For the sandy carrots, use a juicer to make carrot juice. Then cut the sandy carrots as finely as possible and cook them in the carrot juice and a touch of salted water. Blend the cooked carrots with a spoonful of harissa and the fresh juice of one orange.

To serve, cook the barley in salted water until it is al dente. In a pan, mix the barley, a spoonful of harissa, some dried capers, almonds, grapes (dried or fresh), fried shallots and lemon zest. Then sprinkle with fresh pomegranate seeds, salt and pepper.

Photography by @KatieWilsonFoto

ROAST POUSSIN STUFFED WITH COUS COUS, SERVED WITH A FENNEL SALAD, NIGELLA FLATBREADS & YOGHURT

Donated by Damian Clisby at Petersham Nurseries
@damian_clisby @PetershamNurseries

Serves 2

For the poussin

1 poussin, with the wishbone removed
125g giant cous cous, cooked
50g raisins, soaked in water for 20 minutes
25g pistachio nuts, chopped
20g mint, chopped
20g parsley, chopped
5g rose petals, dried
1 preserved lemon skin, chopped
1 lemon
5g rosemary, chopped
25ml olive oil
salt, to taste

For the salad

1 fennel, finely shaved
seeds and juice of ½ pomegranate
20 mint leaves
20 flat-leaf parsley leaves
juice of 1 lemon
salt, to taste

For the flatbread

500g strong bread flour
10g salt
10g yeast
350ml water
25g melted butter
a good pinch of nigella seeds
rock salt
semolina

I think that there is more than enough meat here to share for two, and we should all really be actively trying to eat more vegetables and less meat in consideration of both our health and the planet. This flatbread recipe will make a little more than you need. You can keep the dough in the fridge for the following day.

For the flatbread, begin by crumbling the yeast into the flour, mixing thoroughly, and then add the salt and the water. Using an electric mixer with a dough hook, mix the dough for 10-14 minutes. When it is ready, the dough should come together and leave the bowl with clean sides. Leave the dough in the bowl, covered with a damp cloth, and let it rest for an hour.

To make the bread, preheat your oven to 240C/475F/gas 9 with a heavy roasting tray or ideally a pizza stone inside. Break off golf ball-sized pieces of dough from the main piece. As many or as little as you like, keeping the remainder of the dough for the next day. Roll the pieces to approximately 5mm thick, in any shape you like. Brush with the melted butter and sprinkle generously with the salt and nigella seeds. Place your bread on to a flat tray with no lip that has been dusted lightly with semolina. To cook, slide the tray into the oven and bake for 6-8 minutes.

The poussin needs to be removed from the fridge 40 minutes before cooking. This is because the meat will cook far better from room temperature than it will when it is fridge-cold.

Preheat your oven to 200/400F/gas 6. Mix all the other poussin ingredients together with your cooked cous cous in a bowl, holding back a pinch of both the pistachio nuts and the rose petals to garnish once the bird is cooked. Season the mix to taste with the olive oil, salt and lemon juice.

Fill the poussin with the seasoned cous cous. Drizzle the remainder of the olive oil over the bird, then season with the chopped rosemary and salt. Cook the bird for 25 minutes, then cover and allow to rest for 10 minutes before serving.

For the salad, cut the pomegranate in half and hold it over a large bowl. Bash the back of the fruit with a wooden spoon, allowing the seeds and juice to be caught in the bowl. Add to this the finely shaved fennel, lemon juice, and season to taste with salt.

Once happy with the seasoning, throw in the mint and parsley leaves. The key to this salad is that it is zingy and crunchy. So make it at the last minute just before serving.

Photography by @KatieWilsonFoto

SEARED PIGEON BREAST WITH BEETROOT, HARISSA & LABNEH

Donated by Oliver Rowe
@Oliver_Rowe_London

Serves 4

1 large tub plain yoghurt
2 cloves garlic
½ tsp fennel seed
½ tsp coriander seeds
1 splash white wine
8 pigeon breasts, skin removed
2-3 medium beetroots, skin left on
100ml red wine vinegar
1 tsp fine salt
1 handful salt
1 handful sugar
2 bay leaves
4 plums, halved and de-stoned
30g butter
1 tbsp honey
1 small red onion, finely diced
½ pomegranate
2-3 tbsp fruit syrup
4 tbsp harissa, homemade or bought
extra-virgin olive oil
sea salt
black pepper

Both pigeon and beetroot are common to British and Middle Eastern cuisine, so this recipe represents an exciting culinary blend of the cultures coming together.

First, mix the yoghurt with the fine salt and hang in a tea towel over a bowl. Leave for at least 4 hours, or overnight.

Crush the garlic with a good pinch of salt, the fennel seed and the coriander seed in a pestle and mortar. Mix in the wine and 1 tbsp of olive oil. Rub well into the pigeon breasts, cover and chill for at least 1 hour.

Prepare the harissa if making it yourself. To do this, carefully toast the coriander, cumin and caraway seeds over a medium heat in a dry frying pan until fragrant. Work to a fine powder in a pestle and mortar or a spice grinder.

Add the chillies, pepper and/or sun-dried tomatoes, garlic and salt, then grind to a fine paste.

Stir with remaining ingredients, making sure that there is enough oil to make the paste glossy, then set the harissa aside for at least 1 hour before using.

Next, put the cleaned beetroot into a pan and cover with water, add 75ml of the vinegar, a handful of salt, the sugar and the bay leaves. Cook until tender – about an hour to an hour and a half. Leave to cool in their water until easily handled, then slide the skin off, slice and toss in a bowl with the rest of the vinegar, 75ml of oil, a pinch of salt and some pepper.

In a frying pan, heat a tablespoon of oil, season the pigeon breasts and then cook over a high heat until coloured on the outside – just a minute or so on each side. Set aside to rest.

Clean the pan and melt the honey and butter together. When bubbling and starting to colour, add the plums cut-side down. Fry together until the plums have caramelised a little, turn for a second and remove from the pan.

Arrange the beetroot on plates and slice the pigeon breasts. Place over the beetroot with the caramelised plums, a tablespoon of harissa and a tablespoon of labneh. Drizzle with the fruit syrup, and scatter with the red onion and pomegranate.

Photography by @Joe_Woodhouse

SPICED QUAIL, MAQLUBA, FENNEL, POMEGRANATE & MINT SALAD

Donated by Paradise Garage

@Paradise254

"It's just incredible that so many people in hospitality are getting behind the idea. As long as we can raise as much as we can for the cause that's great. We know it's small but we also know that every little helps, and once we combine all of these fantastic restaurants in London the total will hopefully be really impactful and, most importantly, make a positive difference."

Serves 4

4 whole quails

For the spice marinade

1 tbsp black peppercorns
2 cloves
½ tbsp fennel seeds
½ tbsp cumin seeds
1 small star anise
¼ tsp cardamom pods
¼ cinnamon stick
¼ tsp fenugreek seeds
¼ tsp ginger, ground
½ tbsp sweet paprika
½ tbsp sumac
¼ nutmeg, grated
½ tbsp maldon sea salt
15g ginger, grated
2 cloves garlic, grated
30ml lemon juice
60ml vegetable oil
20g coriander, chopped

For the maqluba

200g jasmine rice
1 large onion
1 whole cinnamon stick
4 cardamom pods
¼ tsp mace
a pinch of cayenne pepper
2 tbsp pomegranate molasses
100ml vegetable oil
½ tsp turmeric
¼ tsp cinnamon, ground
¼ tsp black pepper, ground
50g flaked almonds, toasted
2 large potatoes

To garnish

1 fennel head
1 pomegranate
½ bunch mint
juice of 1 lemon
50ml olive oil
4 tbsp natural yoghurt

We learned how to let bold, punchy flavours sing proudly in our adapted maqluba, matched with quail from Norfolk and marinating it to harness more flavour and spice

Toast all the whole spices gently in a dry pan, then grind in a spice grinder. Mix together with all of the remaining marinade ingredients. Marinate the quails overnight, then roast at 180C/350F/gas 4 until cooked but still slightly pink inside. For the maqluba, rinse the rice, then soak in lightly salted water for 2 hours. Slice the onion and sweat in olive oil with the cinnamon stick, cardamom pods, mace and cayenne pepper. Cook until the onions are caramelised. Add the pomegranate molasses, then cook for another 5 minutes. Set aside.

Once the rice has soaked, drain it and cook in a pan of boiling salted water with a tbsp of olive oil for 7 minutes. Drain and rinse, then mix through the onion mixture and the toasted almonds.

Peel the potatoes and cut into ½ cm-thick slices. Heat up the vegetable oil with the turmeric, ground cinnamon and pepper in an ovenproof dish with a tight-fitting lid. Once the spices start to toast, add 100ml of water and emulsify the mixture. Remove two-thirds of the emulsion and layer the sliced potatoes so that they cover the bottom of the pan. Cook for 3 minutes, and then add the rice on top.

Using the handle of a wooden spoon, gently make 6 holes in the rice to allow it to cook more evenly. Pour the remaining oil and spice mix over the rice and cook on a medium heat for another 3 minutes. Cover the top of the rice with parchment paper, put the lid on and cook in a low oven at 120C/250F/gas ½ for at least 3 hours. Once cooked, allow to cool slightly and then remove the lid and place a plate upside down over the top of the pan. Turn the dish out on to the plate.

To garnish, slice the fennel finely, remove the seeds from the pomegranate, and mix in the mint leaves. Make a dressing with the lemon juice and olive oil. Serve 1 quail per person with a portion of the rice, the dressed salad and a tablespoon of yoghurt.

Photography by @PatriciaNiven

Baked treats

Cakes & tarts

Jams & jellies

Puddings to share

6. SWEETS & DESSERTS

"We're a nation of tea and cake lovers and what better way to do a bit for charity than through making cake. It says so much, and feels relevant – the act of giving and sharing. Hopefully it'll inspire people to hold coffee mornings and continue to raise money and awareness."

Georgina Hayden

BARAZEK (SESAME & PISTACHIO COOKIES) V

Donated by Dalia Dogmoch Soubra
@DaliasKitchen

"Both my parents are Syrian but moved to Europe to provide a better future their children due to the lack of opportunity in Syria. I am grateful every day for their move, that would have been very different for us had they stayed. I grew up between both worlds, being Syrian but living in the West. Food was always my comfort zone and a way that I could share my heritage with those around me. As I grew older, I started noticing that food is a peaceful yet powerful tool to bring people closer to one another."

Makes approximately 30 cookies

For the cookies

150g icing sugar, sifted
130ml clarified butter (or soft butter)
250g flour, sifted
100ml warm water
½ tsp active dried yeast
200g crushed pistachios
400g toasted sesame seeds

For the syrup

250ml water
200g white sugar
3 tbsp honey

Barazek is a famous Syrian dessert from the Midan area. This eggless, crispy cookie is delicately thin and usually comes in tightly packed boxes from renowned Syrian bakeries. My mother used to wait for the barazek cart outside of school and break the larger-sized cookie into several pieces, which she would share with her siblings and friends. I experimented with several recipes until I developed this one, where the texture is just like I remember from the infamous Semiramis bakery in Syria. Once you start with these, you can't stop at one cookie – they are truly addictive.

In a saucepot, add the water, sugar and honey and bring to a simmer. Stir a few times, remove from the heat and let it cool.

Preheat the oven to 170C/325F/gas 3.

Using an electric mixer, cream the sugar and butter together.

Mix the warm water with the yeast and let it sit for a minute.

Add the flour to the butter and sugar mix, then the water and yeast mix, and combine until you obtain a smooth dough which will be quite sticky.

In a bowl, mix the sesame seeds with half the cooled syrup then place the seeds on a plate. Add more syrup if desired.

Prepare another plate with the crushed pistachios.

Using your fingers, dip the sticky dough in the pistachio plate first, then flip the cookie and dip it in the sesame seeds. The dough will be a little tricky but manageable. The stickier it is the better the consistency of the cookie later, but you may add a little more flour if needed.

Place the cookies on a baking tray lined with parchment paper, and bake in the oven for about 20-25 minutes, making sure they are golden brown. Let them cool on a tray and store in a tin or a jar in a dry place.

Photography by @SukainaRajabali

TAHINI, CARDAMOM & DATE CINNAMON ROLLS V

Donated by Izy Hossack
@IzyHossack

"Through my research of Syrian cuisine to create recipes for #CookForSyria, I found lots of my favourite ingredients! Smoky aubergine, coriander, dates and pomegranate – just to name a few."

Makes 10 rolls

For the dough

280ml milk or non-dairy milk, to make vegan, plus a little extra for brushing
2 tsp fast-action dried yeast
50g granulated sugar
220g plain flour, plus extra for kneading
220g wholemeal flour
80g vegetable oil, plus a bit more for the bowl
1 tsp salt

For the filling

60g olive or rapeseed oil (or melted butter if you're not vegan)
3 tbsp tahini paste
70g light brown sugar
2 tsp cinnamon, ground
½ tsp green cardamom, ground
a pinch of salt
100g pitted dates roughly chopped
2 tbsp sesame seeds

I'm a cinnamon roll addict, of course, and always love to find new ways to flavour them. I'd usually have some dried fruit and nuts in a cinnamon roll, so they were easy to substitute for sticky dates and a sprinkle of sesame seeds added a toasty boost of flavour. I used tahini instead of butter which added flavour and a creamy texture.

In a small pot, heat the milk over a low heat until just steaming. Pour into a bowl and leave to cool until only slightly warm. Stir the yeast into the milk and set aside for 5 minutes.

Using your hands, mix the sugar, oil, salt and both the flours into the milk to form a rough dough. Tip the contents of the bowl out onto a clean work surface and knead until smooth and slightly sticky – about 10 minutes – dusting with a little extra flour as needed.

Pour a bit more extra oil into the same bowl that you were using, place the dough into it and turn to coat with oil. Cover with clingfilm and set aside in a warm place for 1 hour - 1½ hours, until doubled in volume.

Dust the work surface with flour again, tip the risen dough out on to it and dust the dough with some flour as well. Roll out into a 35cm square using a floured rolling pin, or even a wine bottle.

Mix the tahini and olive oil and brush over the surface of the dough. Mix the sugar, cinnamon, cardamom and salt, then sprinkle over the surface of the dough in an even layer.

Scatter over the chopped dates and sesame seeds then roll the dough up into a tight log.

Cut into 10 equal pieces and place on to a lined baking tray. Cover with an oiled piece of clingfilm or a clean kitchen towel and then set aside in a warm place to rise for 30-45 minutes, until doubled in size. Preheat the oven to 180C/350F/ gas 4.

Once the rolls have risen, remove the clingfilm and brush with milk using a pastry brush.

Bake for 20-25 minutes until golden. Leave to cool slightly before eating.

Photography by @IzyHossack
Portrait by Bea Duncan

MRASHAM (FLUFFY TURMERIC & YOGHURT BISCUITS) V

Donated by Itab Azzam and Dina Mousawi of Syria Recipes From Home
@ItabAzzam @DMousawi @Syria_RecipesFromHome

Makes approximately 15 biscuits

250g plain flour
125g sugar
10 tbs melted butter
5 tbs room temperature yoghurt
1/2 tsp instant yeast
a pinch of bicarbonate of soda
2 tsp ground turmeric
2 tsp nigella seeds
1 tsp aniseeds
1/2 tsp of cardamom
1/2 tsp nutmeg
1/2 tsp caraway seeds

These are different from what most people are used to in a biscuit. They are fluffy rather than crunchy. This type with turmeric biscuit is mainly made in southern Syria, although different varieties are made all over the country. Syrian Christians call them Easter biscuits as it is mainly made then.

Heat the oven to 180C/350F.

Mix all the dry ingredient together then add the melted butter and rub the mixture with your hands.

After all the butter is absorbed and mixed in well with the flour, add the yoghurt and knead the dough until it forms a uniformed smooth texture. Cover the bowl with a tea towel and leave to rise in a warm place for half an hour.

Roll the dough on a clean kitchen top or a table until achieving half a centimetre thickness. Cut into the shape you desire. Usually in Syria we would use special wooden moulds but if you don't have those you can use ordinary cutters.

Bake in the oven for 10-12 minutes.

Photography by @KatieWilsonFoto
Styling by @KloellaDeville
With thanks to Backgrounds Prop Hire

ROSE BAKLAVA V

Donated by Lily Vanilli
@Lily_Vanilli_Cake

- 4-5 filo pastry sheets
- 80g butter, melted but not hot
- 2 handfuls walnuts, crushed to a near-paste
- 3 tbsp brown sugar
- 10g white sesame
- 100g light brown sugar
- 200ml water
- a handful of culinary rose petals (plus extra, crushed, for optional decoration)

One of our best-loved pastries in the bakery is the rose apple tart, and I wanted to put our twist on the traditional Syrian baklava.

Combine the walnuts, brown sugar and sesame in a bowl and set aside.

Make the syrup by bringing the water, sugar and roses to a boil in a heavy-bottomed saucepan until the sugar has dissolved and is just starting to thicken. Scoop out the petals and discard. Preheat the oven to 180C/350F/gas 4.

Cut your filo lengthways into pieces approximately 5cm deep. While you are working on one piece of filo dough, place the rest under a damp (but not wet) tablecloth to prevent it from drying out.

Place one long strip of filo on your work counter, brush it with melted butter and fill the upper half with some of the mixture, spreading it all the way across the length of the pastry.

Now fold up the bottom half and press it flat and as smooth as possible. Brush the top of the fold with more butter and roll it from left to right to form a rose shape.

Repeat to make all your roses and bake for 20 minutes, or until they are just browning and the pastry is baked. I baked mine in a greased mini cupcake pan, but they should stay put if you bake freeform.

Brush them with some of the syrup while still hot, and then allow to cool completely.

I dusted my finished roses with crushed rose petals.

Photography by @CharlotteHuCo
Portrait by @AliceWhitby

PISTACHIO & POMEGRANATE MOLASSES MA'AMOUL SHORTBREAD PASTRIES V

Donated by Lily Vanilli
@Lily_Vanilli_Cake

Makes around 12

For the dough

120g unsalted butter, softened

½ tsp mahleb powder (an aromatic spice made from cherry seeds)

3 tbsp light brown sugar

250g plain white flour, sifted

2 tbsp milk

For the filling

2 handfuls pistachios, blitzed or crushed to a near-paste

3 tbsp light brown sugar

a few tsp pomegranate molasses

white sesame seeds

100g icing sugar (I mixed mine with crushed, dehydrated raspberry powder)

I love pomegranate molasses and always put them on anything savoury I can, so I was curious to try them out in a sweet. They are the perfect balance of tangy, sour and sweet. You will need a ma'amoul mould for this recipe.

For the dough, beat the butter in a stand mixer for around 4-5 minutes. Beat in the sugar in the final stages. Add the mahleb, then the flour and milk in increments until you have a dough that is not wet, but does not crack as you knead a small piece in your hand. Wrap in clingfilm and chill for 30 minutes.

For the filling, combine the pistachios and sesame seeds to taste, then add the molasses very slowly, mixing in between additions until you have a paste that is spreadable but not wet.

Preheat the oven to 180C/350F/gas 4 and line a baking tray with baking parchment.

Dust your mould with flour. Take a piece of the dough and roll it to a ball, flatten it in your palm and gently press it into the mould. Fill the cavity with the filling and then cover the base with more dough to seal it. Tap the mould on the work counter to release it, it should pop out smoothly. Repeat until all the dough is used up.

Now transfer to a baking tray and bake for 12-15 minutes. To check if your ma'amoul are done, take a look at the bases, they should be just browning, while the rest of the pastry should be white.

Dust the baked and cooled biscuits with icing sugar (adding raspberry powder for colour is optional).

Photography by @CharlotteHuCo
Portrait by @AliceWhitby

BARAZEK SHORTBREADS (BLACK & WHITE SESAME & PISTACHIO BISCUITS) V

Donated by Lily Vanilli
@Lily_Vanilli_Cake

"What was most moving in my research was that the flavours, ingredients and the pastries themselves are so familiar and readily available here in London."

Makes 15 large shortbreads

300g wholemeal flour
75g caster sugar
25g light brown sugar
a pinch of sea salt
a pinch of vanilla
250g very cold unsalted butter, cubed
1 egg yolk
1 egg white
a handful of pistachios, crushed
a handful of black and white sesame seeds, toasted lightly in a hot saucepan for 2 minutes, or until starting to pop

I love the traditional barazek biscuit, and wanted to merge the Syrian flavours with a traditional English biscuit.

Sift the flour, sugars and salt together in a large bowl. Add the cold butter and rub with your fingertips to form fine breadcrumbs. Add the egg yolk and vanilla and bring the mixture together into a dough, being careful not to overwork it.

Roll out on a floured surface to approximately 1cm thick. Cut into any shape you like (I used an 8cm cookie cutter), place on a baking tray lined with parchment, and refrigerate for a minimum of 2 hours, but preferably overnight.

Preheat the oven to 180C/350F/gas 4. Gently brush one side of each cookie with egg white and dust with the crushed pistachios, then do the same on the other side with the sesame. Bake for approximately 12 minutes, or until the edges are just starting to brown. Remove from the oven and allow to cool completely before eating.

Photography by @CharlotteHuCo
Portrait by @AliceWhitby

CHOCOLATE, TAHINI & HONEY CELEBRATION CAKE V

Donated by Georgina Hayden
@GeorgiePuddingNPie

"We're a nation of tea and cake lovers and what better way to do a bit for charity than through making cake. It says so much, and feels relevant – the act of giving and sharing. Hopefully it'll inspire people to hold coffee mornings and continue to raise money and awareness."

Serves 16

- 550g butter
- 125g chocolate
- 185g soft light brown sugar
- 75g caster sugar
- sea salt
- 5 large eggs
- 1 tsp good-quality vanilla extract
- 75g ground almonds
- 150g wholemeal self-raising flour
- 100g rye or wholemeal flour
- 1¼ tsp baking powder
- ½ tsp bicarbonate of soda
- 2 packets sesame snaps
- 600g icing sugar
- 4 tbsp tahini
- 125g honey
- black sesame seeds, to decorate

I took a chocolate celebration cake from my book, Stirring Slowly, as it is a crowd-pleaser, and not too difficult to do ,and I tweaked it. Gone is the sea salt caramel ripple, and instead it is laced with a tahini buttercream. Tahini and chocolate work beautifully together, in a way that many people might not initially think.

Grease and line the base of a springform 20cm cake tin. Preheat the oven to 180C/350F/gas 4, then place a large pan on a low heat and pour in 125ml water. Dot in 250g of the butter and break in the chocolate. Add the soft light brown sugar, caster sugar and a pinch of salt. Melt over a low heat and whisk until smooth. Remove the pan from the hob and leave to cool for 12-15 minutes before whisking in the eggs, vanilla and ground almonds.

In a large mixing bowl, whisk together the flours, baking powder and bicarbonate of soda. Then slowly pour into the molten chocolate mixture, whisking constantly until you have a smooth batter. Pour the mixture into the cake tin and pop in the oven for 55 minutes. When done, leave in the tin for 10 minutes, then transfer to a cooling rack and leave to cool completely. When cooled, cut off the top if it has peaked a little (keep this to one side for decorating). Slice into 3 equal layers.

Make the buttercream by beating the remaining 300g butter in a freestanding mixer until pale and creamy. Sift in half the icing sugar and beat until smooth, then repeat with the remaining icing sugar. Beat for a further 4 minutes, then add the tahini and 50g of honey, and beat for 1 more minute, until smooth.

To layer your cake, dot a little buttercream on a cake stand and place one of the layers on top. Spoon on a quarter of the buttercream and use a spatula to level it. Drizzle with a little honey, sprinkle over a layer of the smashed sesame snaps and top with the second sponge. Repeat, then top with the final sponge. Finish the cake by covering with the remaining buttercream and rippling in the remaining honey to give a marbled effect.

Sprinkle the remaining sesame snaps around the edge of the cake, along with the black sesame seeds, and crumble over any extra sponge. For an even more opulent finish, dust with a little edible gold dust or leaf.

Photography by @CharlotteHuCo

FIG & ALMOND BAKLAVA TART V

Donated by Chetna Makan
@ChetnaMakan

"Syrian sweets are very similar to Indian sweets in that both Indian and Syrian sweets use sugar or syrups, a lot of dry fruits and nuts. There are also a lot of milk-based desserts in both the cuisines."

Serves 4-6

8 ripe figs
2 tbsp clear honey
150g unsalted butter, softened
150g golden caster sugar
150g ground almonds
2 large eggs
30g walnuts, finely chopped
30g pistachios, finely chopped
6 sheets filo pastry
60g melted unsalted butter

To finish
a handful of pistachios
a few drops of clear honey

This is a beautiful dish with amazing flavours inspired by the baklava, which is one of my favourite sweets to eat. I have used the filo pastry for the tart which is essential to baklava, and also has a delicious layer of nuts at the bottom of the tart. This is then topped with frangipane, which enhances the nutty flavour, and the tart is then topped with honey, which finishes the tart beautifully.

Heat the oven to 180C/350F/gas 4. Cut the figs in half and then place them cut-side up on a roasting tray. Brush them with the honey and bake for 10-12 minutes until just soft.

To make the frangipane, cream the butter and sugar until light and fluffy, which takes roughly 2 minutes. Add the almonds and eggs and mix it all well.

Grease a 23cm tart tin and place a sheet of filo inside it. Brush generously with melted butter followed by another sheet of filo, leaving the sides hanging. Repeat the same with the 4 other sheets.

Sprinkle the chopped nuts on the base of the tart, followed by the frangipane. Now place the roasted figs carefully on the frangipane and gently fold the hanging pastry on top, one layer at a time. Brush it all well with some butter and finish by sprinkling some nuts on top. Bake for 35-40 minutes.

Remove from the tin and place on the serving plate. Drizzle some honey on top and enjoy this warm.

Photography by @PatriciaNiven

OLIVE OIL & PISTACHIO CAKE WITH YOGHURT SORBET V

Donated by Angela Hartnett at Cafe Murano
@AngelaCooking

"It's so important to support this cause – especially when you see the heartbreaking pictures in the news and read what is going on. Our #CookForSyria dish is something easy to replicate at home and incorporates much-loved ingredients and subtle spices used in Syrian cuisine."

Serves 8-10

For the olive oil & pistachio cake

100g plain flour, sifted
5 tsp baking powder
200g ground almonds
50g pistachio nuts
400g sugar
500ml olive oil
10 eggs, lightly beaten
zest of 2 lemons
zest of 2 oranges
1 tsp cinnamon, ground
1 tsp cardamom, ground
nutmeg, grated
20cm/8in round cake tin

For the yoghurt sorbet

95g sugar
17.5g glucose
165g water
400g greek yoghurt
30g lemon juice
100g pistachio nuts

The cake is a recipe we have used before and have adapted by adding some spices that are typical to Syrian cuisine. Syrians are subtle with their use of spice in cooking rather than heavy. We included pistachios, cinnamon, cardamom and orange zest. It's meant to be eaten, similar to many Arabic cuisines, in a huge family style, which I like.

Preheat the oven to 160C/325F/gas 3. Line a rectangular baking tin with greaseproof paper.

Mix all of the dry ingredients together into a bowl, then add the eggs, olive oil and zest. Whisk together into a smooth, batter-like consistency. Pour into the baking tin and cook for 50 minutes, or until a skewer comes out clean.

Allow to cool and remove from the tin.

Serve with pistachio and yoghurt sorbet, and pomegranate or raspberry compote.

For the sorbet, boil the water and the sugars and then remove from the heat.

Whisk in the yoghurt and the lemon juice, then fold in 100g of pistachio nuts and freeze in a paco jet machine or an ice-cream maker. (If using an ice-cream maker, add another 60g of caster sugar to the mixture.)

Photography by @KatieWilsonFoto

PISTACHIO & NUTMEG CAKE V

Donated by Stevie Parle at Dock Kitchen
@StevieParle @Dock_Kitchen

Serves 8

150g pistachios, finely ground
75g pistachios,
coarsely chopped
200g ground almonds
220g soft brown sugar
120g butter, softened
1 tsp salt
2 eggs, lightly beaten
250g greek-style yoghurt
1 tbsp freshly grated nutmeg
1 tsp baking powder
yoghurt, rose petals and pomegranate seeds to serve

This classic Dock Kitchen cake is based on a traditional Syrian recipe. The bold quantity of nutmeg gives the cake a wonderful musty, savoury note that few can identify.

Preheat oven to 180C/350F/gas 4. Line a 20cm springform cake tin with two layers of baking paper.

Mix ground pistachios, almonds, sugar, butter and salt with a wooden spoon. Spread a little under half over the bottom of the lined tin.

Combine the remaining mixture with the eggs, yoghurt, nutmeg and baking powder. Beat until creamy. Pour into the pan and scatter with chopped pistachios.

Bake until golden for between 45 minutes - 1 hour.

Serve sprinkled with pomegranate seeds, a blob of yoghurt and a few rose petals, fresh or dried if you have them.

Photography by @Joe_Woodhouse

ORANGE, ALMOND & PISTACHIO CAKE WITH POMEGRANATE ROSE JEWEL SYRUP V

Donated by Henrietta Inman
@HenriettaInman

"This campaign brings awareness in a whole new way which is through food, a universal necessity and part of the identity of every country. Syrian food celebrates their rich and diverse culture and this project, with its evocation of our senses through food, allows us to really take note of what has happened in Syria and to stop and help."

Serves 8

For the orange cake

500g oranges (around 3)
4 eggs
150g coconut sugar
225g ground almonds
1 tsp rosewater
1 tsp baking powder
50g pistachio nuts, toasted and roughly chopped, plus extra to decorate

For the pomegranate rose jewel syrup

150g pomegranate juice, unsweetened
40g honey
15g pomegranate molasses
4 tsp rosewater
1 pomegranate

Nuts are used extensively in Syrian cooking. Pistachios and almonds are some of the most popular, with the former having been grown in Syria for thousands of years. They add a slight crunch and a hint of green to this soft, syrupy and fragrant orange cake.

Cook the oranges in their skins by placing them in a lidded saucepan and covering them with cold water. Bring the water to a boil, then turn down to a low heat and simmer for 2 hours, topping up the water when necessary, until the fruit is soft and a skewer pierces it easily. Drain and leave to cool.

Preheat the oven to 180C/350F/gas 4. Grease the bottom and sides of a 20cm springform cake tin, then line the base with baking parchment. Cut the cooled oranges in half, remove any pips and blitz the whole fruit, including their skin, in a food processor until they form a smooth pulp.

Add the rest of the ingredients except the pistachio nuts to the food processor, and process until the mixture is completely smooth and well combined. Add the pistachios and pulse a few times.

Pour the mix into the prepared tin and bake for 20 minutes. Rotate the cake in the oven and bake for a further 20 minutes, then reduce the heat to 160C/325F/gas 3 and bake for another 20 minutes, or until a skewer inserted into the centre of the cake comes out clean. Remove from the oven and leave to cool completely in the tin.

Then make the pomegranate rose jewel syrup. Place all the ingredients, except for the rosewater and the pomegranate seeds, in a small saucepan. Bring to a boil and lower the heat to a rolling boil for 5 minutes.

Remove from the heat, add the rosewater and when the cake is still warm, pierce it with a skewer and pour over the syrup, leaving a couple of tablespoons in the pan. Break open the pomegranate and remove the seeds over the pan, letting any of the juice fall into the syrup. Mix to coat the seeds in the remaining liquid.

Once the cake has cooled, remove from the tin, transfer to a plate and pour over the syrup and pomegranate seeds mixture. Decorate with rose petals, chopped pistachios and serve. It's delicious with natural yoghurt or crème fraîche. The cake will keep well in the fridge for five days and freezes well for up to a month.

Photography by @KatieWilsonFoto

A JELLY OF STRAWBERRIES, ROSÉ & ROSES V

Donated by Thane Prince
@ThanePrince

Makes approximately 5 jellies
Keeps for 6 months

500g ripe strawberries

750ml rosé wine

700g jam sugar
(sugar with pectin)

1 tsp citric acid
or 2 tablespoons lemon juice

2 tbsp rosewater

4 tbsp dried rose petals

Pretty as a picture, this jelly is made using a bottle of rosé wine. Wine jellies are delicious and can be made quite easily using a variety of wines, whether red, white or rosé. This one is a fragrant blend of pink wine and strawberries, a summer treat if ever I saw one – or perhaps the best Valentine's Day breakfast ever. Should you want to make jellies using other wines, choose a full-flavoured one: shiraz for red and a good oaky chardonnay for white-wine jellies. I have used a granache rosé here, a good deep pink one. You'll need to add some acid as well as pectin, so I've used citric acid and jam sugar. Dried Persian rose petals can be bought at many places now, but you could dry your own if you have a rose garden. The petals float to the top of the jelly.

Begin by preparing the fruit. Remove the stems and then wash the berries, shaking the water from them. Put the berries into a blender or a food processor. Whiz until you have a puree.

Pour the wine into a heavy-bottomed saucepan. Add the strawberry puree and warm the mixture over a low heat for about 3-4 minutes. Leave to infuse for 1 hour.

Set up your jelly bag, and spoon in the mixture, allowing it to drip overnight.

The next day, put a small plate in the freezer. Put 4-5 clean jars into an oven heated to 100C/200F/gas 2. Pour the juice into a clean pan and add the sugar and citric acid.

Place this over a low heat and cook gently, stirring until the sugar has fully dissolved and there is no grittiness left in the pan or on the spoon.

Turn up the heat and bring to a full rolling boil, one that can't be stirred down. Cook for 5 minutes.

Now turn off the heat and test for a set. To do this, spoon a small amount of jelly on to one of the small plates that you've taken from the freezer. If, after about a minute, when the jelly has cooled slightly, the surface wrinkles as you push gently with your finger, then you are ready to continue. If not, re-boil for a further 2 minutes, then switch off and test again.

Once you are happy the jelly will set, turn off the heat and skim off any scum that has collected on the surface of the jelly using the slotted spoon, washing it between skims.

Stir in the rosewater and the rose petals and then allow the jelly to sit for 10 minutes. Stir again, place the pan back on the heat and bring gently up to boiling point. Then take the pan from the heat and leave for 5 minutes. Pot the jelly into the hot jars, cover with lids and leave to cool. When the jars are cold, check the lids are tight and store in a cool dark place.

Photography by Steve Lee, courtesy of Dorling Kindersley
Portrait by @JamesKemmenoe

FIG AND ORANGE-BLOSSOM JAM V

Donated by Kylee Newton
@NewtonAndPott

"Because I was concentrating on the sweeter side of Syrian cuisine I wanted to use figs where I discovered that Syria is one of the natural habitats of the fruit trees - and from there they were transported to the rest of the world."

Makes 3-4 228ml jars

1.5kg figs
75ml water
30ml lemon juice
600g granulated sugar
zest of ½ orange
25ml orange-blossom water
filo pastry

To serve
pistachios, chopped
mascarpone
orange zest

I wanted to make a Fig jam, as figs feel exotic and are naturally sweet without having to add too much sugar. The Orange Blossom seemed apt to bring in the flavours of Syria – then just add filo and pistachios like a deconstructed Baklawa.

Wash your jars in hot, soapy water and rinse well with hot water. Drip-dry upside down to remove excess water, and then place in an oven heated to 100C for about 20 minutes to sterilise.

Wash and cut the figs into 8 pieces, then place in a large pan with the water and lemon juice. Soften the fruit on a low-medium heat for about 10 minutes.

Add the zest and sugar to the pan and bring to a boil, stirring to dissolve the sugar. Once the sugar has dissolved, boil rapidly for 15-20 minutes, until the figs have thickened and become sticky. They should leave a trail with your wooden spoon when dragged across the bottom of the pan.

Once at the desired consistency, skim off any scum that has formed and ladle into your warm sterilised jars. Once cooled, seal, date and label.

Use within 6 months and once the seal is broken, refrigerate and eat within 3-4 weeks.

For the filo jam flowers, layer 4-5 filo pastry squares, staggering the corners to look like a star or petals, in a well-greased mini muffin tin.

Dollop a large teaspoon of the fig and orange-blossom jam (the size of the dollop should be dependent on the width of your muffin holes) into the middle of each star and bake in a hot oven for 10-12 minutes.

Serve sprinkled with chopped pistachios and mascarpone mixed with orange zest.

Photography by @KatieWilsonFoto
Styling by @KloellaDeville

HALAWA MA FISTUK HALABI (PISTACHIO HALVA) V

Donated by Itab Azzam and Dina Mousawi of Syria Recipes From Home
@ItabAzzam @DMousawi @Syria_RecipesFromHome

200g sugar
200ml tahini
75ml water
50g pistachios, roughly chopped

In Syria, Halva is called Halawa which in arabic means 'sweetness'. It is eaten all over the Middle East and in Syria with a bit of bread and butter.

You can make your halva with almonds, honey, rose water or any flavour you prefer.

Make the sugar syrup by heating up the sugar and water in a frying pan. Simmer for about 10 mins. The sugar will first dissolve, then begin to bubble and thicken. The longer you leave it, the thicker it will be. You want it to be thinner than the texture of honey, but thicker than water.

Put a handful of pistachios in the bottom of a tuppaware container (or any other flat container).

Once you have made the syrup, remove from the heat, leave for a minute or two to settle. Then add the tahini and stir. Keep stirring for a good 5 minutes until it is thick and almost starts to separate. Mix in the rest of the pistachios. Put all the mixture into the container and firmly press down using a metal spoon. Smooth the top down with the back of the spoon and leave for a couple of hours until it has cooled and set.

Serve with flat bread and a bit of butter, or simply eat on its own as a bit of 'sweetness' after your meal.

Photography by @KatieWilsonFoto
Styling by @KloellaDeville

DATE-BAKED LABNEH, BEETROOT CARDAMOM PUREE, SPICED MERINGUE, HAZELNUT CORIANDER CRISP V

Donated by Mitz Vora at Foley's
@FoleysRestaurant

For the crumble
250g cold butter
250g granulated sugar
250g plain flour
250g hazelnuts, ground
1 tsp cinnamon, ground
½ tsp salt

For the spiced meringue
4 egg whites
225g granulated sugar
½ tsp cardamom, ground
½ tsp cinnamon, ground

For the hazelnut tuille
200g egg whites
12g salt
75g almonds, ground
125g plain flour
200g butter

For the date labneh
415g greek yoghurt, hung overnight
100g condensed milk
175g double cream
125g date molasses

Beetroot and cardamom puree
6 beetroots
3 green cardamom pods
2 tbsp extra-virgin olive oil
½ tsp salt
4 tbsp granulated sugar

To serve
hazelnuts, chopped
coriander seeds, toasted

My research showed me that Syrian cuisine is a melting pot of different cultures from neighbouring countries like Turkey, Lebanon and Iraq. I would say that the Syrian element in my dish are the spices like coriander, cardamom, cinnamon and Labneh cheese.

To make the crumble, dice the chilled butter into small cubes. Put all of the ingredients into a food processor and mix until you get a sand-like texture.

Bake in a preheated oven at 150C/300F/gas 2 for 30 minutes, mixing the crumble every 10 minutes until golden brown.

For the spiced meringue, whip the egg whites until frothy. Gradually add sugar in a steady stream until the egg whites become glossy. Add the spices and whip more until they form stiff peaks.

Scoop the mix into a piping bag and pipe on to a baking sheet lined with parchment paper. Bake at 110C/225F/gas ¼ for an hour.

For the hazelnut tuille, mix the egg whites and the salt until dissolved, then add the ground almonds and flour. Add in the butter slowly and combine. Rest in the fridge for 30 minutes.

Using a spatula, spread the mixture thinly on to a baking sheet lined with parchment paper. Dust with coriander seeds and chopped hazelnuts. Bake for 12 minutes at 180C/350F/gas 4 until golden brown.

For the date labneh, mix all of the ingredients until they form a smooth paste. Scoop the mixture into a shallow baking dish and wrap with aluminium foil. Place the baking dish in a deeper baking tray, and then pour hot water in to this tray. Bake the labneh for 40 min at 120C/250F/gas ½. Allow to cool down to room temperature before chilling it in the fridge.

For the beetroot and cardamom puree, peel and grate the beetroot, then mix with all the other ingredients. Spoon the mixture into a vacuum-pack food sealer bag and seal. Place the bag in simmering water until the beetroot is cooked and soft.

If you don't have vacuum-pack bags, then place all of the ingredients into a casserole dish and cook until the beetroot is soft. Put all of the ingredients in a blender and blend until smooth.

Photography by @KatieWilsonFoto

ROASTED BLACK FIGS, BAKLAVA ICE CREAM & WALNUT BRITTLE V

Donated by Andrew Clarke, pictured, and Jackson Boxer at Brunswick House
@FleurDeLysLdn @Jackson_Boxer @BrunswickHse

"I had seen a baklava milkshake made by Action Bronson once, and figured he was missing a trick."

Serves 4

For the baklava ice cream
500ml double cream
500ml milk
180g caster sugar
200g baklava
7 egg yolks

For the figs
4 black figs, the very best money can buy
1 tbsp pomegranate molasses
1 tbsp fig balsamic vinegar
1 tbsp good-quality honey

For the walnut brittle
250g caster sugar
80g golden syrup
60g water
25g unsalted butter
½ tsp bicarbonate of soda
a pinch of maldon sea salt
200g walnuts, roasted and chopped

For the pistachio purée
300g green pistachios
2 tbsp extra-virgin olive oil
maldon sea salt
water

I've always had a natural love of Middle Eastern cuisine, but I only take influence from it, rather than a traditional approach. An old favourite restaurant of mine was a Syrian place. I must've eaten the whole menu many times over. My dish is a simple showcase of delicious black figs, supported by some delicious nutty, creamy things.

For the baklava ice cream, combine the milk with the baklava and 80g of sugar in a pan and bring to the boil slowly.

Meanwhile, cream the remaining sugar and the egg yolks. Whisk the hot, milky liquid on to the eggs, return to the heat and cook out.

Remove from the heat and add the cream to cool the mix. Pass through fine chinois and cool before churning. For a textured ice cream, you can add 150g of chopped baklava towards the end of the churning.

For the figs, score a cross at the top of each one to expose some of the flesh. Arrange in a small baking dish, allowing for 1cm of space between each piece of fruit.

Mix the molasses, balsamic and honey together and pour over the figs. Bake for 5-6 minutes at 180C/350F/gas 4 until soft but not mushy. Keep warm.

For the walnut brittle, make sure you have a large greaseproof-lined baking tray or a silpat baking mat ready before starting.

Add the sugar, golden syrup and water to a heavy-based saucepan over a gentle heat. Once the sugar has dissolved, add the butter and stir until melted. Increase the temperature and continue to cook until the mixture reaches 150-154C/302-309F.

Remove from the heat and stir in the rest of ingredients well. Pour out on to the baking tray and allow to cool. Chop the walnut brittle into small pieces.

For the pistachio puree, put the nuts into a pressure cooker along with the olive oil and just enough water to cover. Cook for 30 minutes and allow to depressurise.

Transfer the contents to a thermomix (or a food processor) and blitz until a fine puree is achieved. Season with salt and allow to cool. It's not easy to make smaller quantities of this, but it does freeze well and can be used in both sweet and savoury dishes.

To plate, wipe the pistachio puree across the plate and place a pile of walnut brittle just off centre. Top with a scoop of ice cream. The fig halves can be arranged on the other side of the plate, with the roasting juices poured over and around. Add a piece or two of the baklava to finish.

Photography by @PatriciaNiven

ROSE-SCENTED RICE PUDDING V

Donated by Jack Monroe
@MXJackMonroe

When I was asked to get involved with the Cook For Syria project, I agreed immediately. The premise was so simple, so generous, so altruistic, so at odds with the raging war and hateful rhetoric that permeated every conversation about one of the greatest humanitarian crises in our history. It was a project of love and support. As I started to put ideas together, I knew that I wanted to include roses as a symbol of that love, so here they are.

200g plain rice
100g dark-brown sugar
1.2l full-fat milk
100ml rosewater
100ml double cream
a little grated nutmeg
zest and juice of 1 orange
rose petals, to garnish

Rosewater is a classic Middle Eastern ingredient, and one that I use liberally in my own cooking whenever I feel like a gentle, luxurious moment of calm. In popular Western culture, we associate roses with love, and often the giving of roses is a proclamation of affection and appreciation.

This recipe couldn't be simpler, but it does take a long, slow cook to get it just right. First, preheat your oven to 140C/275F/gas 1.

Grab yourself a large ovenproof dish and gently butter the bottom of it. Add the rice, and cover with the milk and the rosewater. Add most of the sugar and stir well.

Grate the orange zest and set to one side to use later. Finely slice the remaining orange and lay on top of the rice – it may disappear into the liquid but will re-emerge at the end as the rice absorbs it and swells.

Cover and place in the centre of the oven. Cook covered for 90 minutes, then remove. Add rose petals, orange zest and grated nutmeg with the remaining sugar, then return to the oven uncovered for 30 minutes to finish and caramelise. Stir in the cream to serve.

Photography by @PatriciaNiven

SPICED ORANGE-BLOSSOM RICE PUDDING WITH DATES, NUTS & SEEDS V

Donated by Mariana and Danny at Jamie Oliver's Fifteen
@MarianaSweets @DannyMcCubbin @JamiesFifteen

"I went to Calais this past Christmas to help the refugee community kitchen cook a Christmas meal, and I was deeply touched by the situation of the people. I met very nice people from Syria, they shared with us their life experiences and how it is living in a country torn apart by war. That experience changed me as a person."

Serves 4-6

For the granola
500g oats
100g oil
300g honey
200g hazelnuts, toasted
200g pistachios, toasted
200g almonds, toasted
50g sunflower seeds
50g pumpkin seeds
50g dates
50g raisins
50g dry apricots
200g honey

For the date and prune purée
100g pitted prunes, diced into small pieces
50g dates, diced into small pieces
2 oranges, juiced
100ml water

For the filo pastry stick
1 packet filo pastry
100g butter, melted
50g sunflower seeds
50g pumpkin seeds
30g pistachios
30g hazelnuts

For the rice pudding
200g pudding rice
2 tbsp orange-blossom water
1.5 litres milk
200ml double cream
250g sugar
1 vanilla pod
1 cinnamon stick
1 tsp clove powder
zest of 2 oranges
edible flowers, for decorating
fresh honeycomb, to serve

Since I was invited to participate in the project I started doing research on Syrian desserts. They have a tradition of eating a type of rice pudding for Christmas and New Year's Eve, In Portugal and Brazil we have the same tradition. Therefore I decided to mix the Luso Portuguese influence with a Syrian twist – lots of nuts, pistachio, orange blossom and flowers.

Mix together the oats, oil, vanilla and honey. Spread out on to a lined baking sheet and bake at 160C/325F/gas 3 until golden brown, mixing every 5-10 minutes so it all cooks evenly.

Blitz together the nuts, seeds and dried fruits. Combine the toasted nuts and the oat mix together with honey, then spread out on to a lined baking sheet. Bake at 150C/300F/gas 2 for 10-15 minutes.

For the purée, simmer the prunes and dates in a saucepan for 10-15 minutes until most of the liquid has been absorbed. Blend until smooth.

For the filo stick, blitz the nuts and seeds into chunks. Preheat the oven at 180C/350F/gas 4 and line a baking tray with greaseproof paper. Melt the butter in a small saucepan. Cut the filo pastry into sheets measuring approximately 10 x 5cm.

Brush the pastry with melted butter and start layering the sheets one by one, brushing butter on to each layer. Use 4-5 layers. Sprinkle the nuts and seeds on top and bake for 10-15 minutes.

For the rice pudding, combine the milk, cream, vanilla, sugar, cinnamon, cloves, ginger and orange zest in a pan, then bring to a boil. Let the milk infuse for about 1 hour and cover. Put the milk infusion and the rice in a pot and cook on a low heat for 30-40 minutes, stirring frequently.

Cover the pot until it has thickened. Add the orange-blossom water. Divide between bowls and serve with the granola, purée, filo pastry and honeycomb.

Photography by @KatieWilsonFoto
Styling by @KloellaDeville

PORTUGUESE RICE PUDDING YABRAK WITH SAFFRON, PISTACHIO & DRUNKEN FIGS (RICE PUDDING WRAPPED IN VINE LEAVES) V

Donated by Antonio Galapito at Taberno Mercado
@AntonioGalapito @TabernaMercado

Makes 15 portions

300g glutinous rice, washed
150g caster sugar
1 litre of milk
30g cornflour
peel of 2 lemons
peel of 2 oranges
½ stick of cinnamon
1g saffron, lightly toasted
15 vine leaves
chopped pistachios, to garnish

For the drunken figs
15 ripe figs
2 litres red wine
1 litre port wine
peel of 4 lemons
peel of 4 oranges
1 stick cinnamon
150g sugar

We were inspired by the use of rice, and the idea of a sweet version of a savoury Syrian dish (yabrak). It's the perfect combination when merged with a traditional Portuguese rice pudding.

Infuse the milk with saffron, cinnamon, sugar, orange and lemon peel. Bring to 90C/195F, and then cover with clingfilm for 40 minutes somewhere cool. Strain and store in a warm place.

Rinse the rice in running water for about 10 minutes. Add the rice together with the warm milk, put in an oven tray covered with clingfilm and steam at 100C/212F for about 45 minutes. Once steamed, uncover and let the rice cool.

To make the drunken figs, mix all the ingredients, and put the figs inside the liquid. Poach at a very low simmer for about 2 hours, being careful not to boil the figs.

Reduce the liquid by about a third, so that it resembles a light wine broth, with plenty of aroma. Set aside for the vine leaves.

For the vine leaves, fill a pot with salted water and brine the 15 vine leaves for 1 hour. Rinse in water for 30 minutes. Then poach the leaves in the remaining fig sauce for 1 hour.

To assemble, take a vine leaf and lay flat, then spoon approximately 2 tablespoons of saffron rice into each leaf. Wrap and roll tightly.

Once all leaves have been rolled, steam everything together until the rice is warmed through.

Serve with the poached figs, coarsely chopped pistachio and finish with 2 spoonfuls of warm fig sauce per person.

Photography by @KatieWilsonFoto

TAHINI AND ORANGE PEEL SEMIFREDDO WITH ROSE & PISTACHIO V

Donated by Jack Monroe
@MXJackMonroe

- 4 large eggs
- 300ml double cream
- 200g caster sugar
- 100g tahini
- 1 large orange
- a pinch of salt
- a fistful of pistachios
- rose petals, to decorate

First, grate the zest from the outside of the orange with a sharp knife, microplane or grater. Set to one side – you'll be needing this later.

Next, line a loaf tin or other small receptacle with two layers of clingfilm, using your fingers to push it into the corners, with a few inches spare all round. This is to make the semifreddo easy to remove later – if you don't have any clingfilm, you can skip this step, but it can get a little messy.

Separate the eggs and refrigerate the whites to use for something else – meringues, cake, an egg white omelette...

Pop the yolks into a large mixing bowl and pour in the sugar, add two thirds of the zest and the salt and tahini, and beat together until the yolks are white and fluffy, and the mixture has doubled in size.

Add the cream and squeeze in the orange juice, and beat well until it forms stiff peaks – I used to have to make this with a friend on hand to take turns at beating it, but I seem to be able to do it all by myself these days! If you have an electric whisk or stand mixer loitering around, now would be a great time to get it out, but if not then it's a labour of love – put some loud music on and get a rhythm going, and it will be done before you know it.

When the cream is light and fluffy and forms soft peaks – and slowly drops off an overturned spoon or fingers – then you're good to go. Pop the remaining zest, pistachios and rose petals into the bottom of the loaf tin and give it a shake to disperse it along the bottom – when turned out, it will sit pretty on the top – get as arty as you like with it, but I just like it flung all over.

Carefully spoon the cream mixture into the loaf tin and give it a gentle shake to get it into all the corners and smooth the top. Carefully fold the clingfilm over the top, and pop in the freezer for at least 4 hours to set.

Photography by @PatriciaNiven

MUHALLABIA (MILK & ORANGE-BLOSSOM PUDDING) V

Donated by Dalia Dogmoch Soubra
@DaliasKitchen

Serves 6

1 litre of milk
100g white sugar
a pinch of salt
50g cornflour
2 tbsp orange blossom
crushed pistachios

Muhalabia is a classic and simple Middle Eastern pudding, similar to a blancmange in France or the Italian panna cotta. It is a very traditional dessert in Syria, and is often served in homes and restaurants. My grandmother used to make this for us often, especially when we were not feeling well, as she believed that it was soothing, and that the milk, sugar and orange blossom gave us a boost of energy. It certainly did, and it still makes me feel better and nostalgic when I have it today.

In a saucepot, bring the milk, sugar and salt to a boil.

Adding a little milk to the cornflour, mix it into a smooth paste before adding it to the milk.

Add the orange blossom next, whisk vigorously and simmer for 10 minutes, stirring constantly until the milk thickens and properly coats the back of the spoon.

Pour the thickened milk into ramekins or serving glasses and place them in the fridge for at least 2 ½ hours to set.

Top with crushed pistachios, a little orange zest and serve.

Photography by @SukainaRajabali

SPECIAL THANKS

We are so grateful to everyone who has supported the #CookForSyria initiative. We would like to thank all those who volunteered their time to cook, photograph, style, design, advise, donate recipes or help in any other way. We couldn't have done it without you.

A huge thank you to all of our amazing contributors who were inspired to create their own recipes for the cause. We loved seeing the spirit of Syrian cuisine come to life through your dishes and have been touched by the stories you've shared and the inspiration behind them.

We would like to give special thanks to:

Our brilliant co-founder Gemma Bell for her wonderful ideas, tireless work and for always managing to keep everyone smiling. We couldn't have partnered with someone better. And her team, Gemma Bell and Company, particularly Alice Grier for spreading the word.

The NEXTGen committee – Linda Blank, CEO (Chief Email Officer) and finance extraordinaire; Shivani Mawji for keeping us all in check when things got a bit nuts. Layla Yarjani and Hortense Decaux, for their patience and support when things needed to be turned around faster than the speed of light.

Our amazing gang of volunteer photographers, Charlotte Hu, Katie Wilson, Patricia Niven and Joe Woodhouse, who have been in and out of restaurants and chefs' homes across London, and editing into the early hours to produce stunning shots.

Dina Mousawi and Itab Azzam of Syria Recipes From Home, Saima Khan, Danny McCubbin, the team who helped at Jamie's Fifteen – Becks Wilkinson, Kim Somauroo, Rosie McCarthy, Maria Paris – and all those who have dedicated their weekends to cooking up a storm. And Chloe Ride for styling the food so artfully.

Our talented designers, Barns Furr, Milly Hill and Alica Jörg, for creating a beautiful brand and a recipe book that anyone would be proud to have in their home or kitchen.

Charlie Brotherstone and Jacq Burns, who guided us when we decided to brave it and go down the self-publishing route for speed, and in order to raise as much money as possible for children of Syria. Rupert Harbour, who got this recipe book into stores around the nation.

Everyone at SUITCASE for their publishing acumen and support in times of madness, alongside our tech team, Alexander Hawkings-Byass and Jojo Regan from BMAS, for building CookForSyria.com in record time. And Codi for your continued technical support.

Sub-editor Lauren York, who spent day and night furiously researching, sub-editing and indexing each and every page, as well as Melissa Hemsley and Chris Keeling for their wise words and input.

Laura Jackson and Alice Levine of Jackson&Levine, for giving us invaluable supper club tips to bring the recipes to life and share them with friends.

Imad Alarnab for donating so much of your time and your Syrian food expertise.

Shilpa Patel, Thomas Sayers and Monica Tanouye from Unicef for help with communication and global support.

Our dear friends and family for their ongoing support throughout the whole journey.

Those who continued efforts in London, Lily Vanilli for the #BakeForSyria initiative and Tommy Tannock, Johnnie Collins and The Store Team for letting us host our launch event and London Food Month in your incredible space.

Everyone who made #CookForSyria happen in cities around the world by hosting supper clubs and events: Pat Nourse, Jeanine Bribosia, The Cru Media, Gemima Cody, Fairfax Media, Sofia Patel, Sofia Vilá in Sydney and Melbourne; Dervla Louli in Hong Kong, Dalia Dogmoch in Dubai; Casey Rotter, Samantha Nicles and Francesco de Flaviis in the United States; Sonia Gaillis-Delepine, Hortense Decaux and Caroline Arditti in Paris; and other volunteers in Barcelona, Amsterdam and Luxembourg.

And finally, we would like to thank all of you around the world who are getting involved, and sharing your experiences, be it in your home, restaurant or even office. We hope that through these recipes, many others will start and continue to #CookForSyria.

INDEX

INDEX

V

VEGETARIAN DISHES (IN BOOK ORDER)

INDEX

CONTRIBUTORS

Published in 2017 by SUITCASE Magazine Ltd

First published in 2016 by SUITCASE Magazine Ltd

Photography by Charlotte Hu, Katie Wilson, Patricia Niven and Joe Woodhouse

Additional photos by: Alice Whiby, Amber Rowlands, Charlotte Hu, David Loftus, Francis Davison, Hannah India Photography, Issy Croker, Izy Hossak, James A. Grant, James Lyndsay, Joe Woodhouse, John Whaite, Katie Wilson, Louis Fernando, Marcus Cobden, Milly Kenny-Ryder, Nicholas Hopper, Oleg Tolstoy, Patricia Niven, Sophia Spring, Steve Lee (courtesy of Dorling Kindersley), Sukaina Rajabali, Symmetry Breakfast, Thomas Bowles, Muse Mohammed/UN Migration Agency

SUITCASE Magazine Ltd Registered in England and Wales No. 07866400

SUITCASE Magazine Ltd Connaught House, 1-3 Mount St, London, W1K 3NB
SUITCASEmag.com
VAT No. 167412115

A CIP catalogue record for this title is available from the British Library

Forest Stewardship Council

Curator: Clerkenwell Boy
Editor: Serena Guen
Art direction: Barns Furr
Designers: Milly Hill, Alica Jörg
Photographers: Charlotte Hu, Joe Woodhouse, Katie Wilson and Patricia Niven
Food stylist: Chloe Ride
Sub-editors: Lauren York, Holly Stevenson and Samantha Sharman

Printed and bound in the UK by CPI Colour

ISBN 978-1- 5272-0334- 1

All profits from this book will support children affected by the crisis in Syria through Unicef's NEXTGeneration London, a fundraising group of Unicef UK. Unicef UK registered charity 1072612 (England and Wales).

CookForSyria.com